Leading While Black

"It is important to understand that Black leadership in North America has always been situated within a racialized context. Fanny Jackson Coppin, Mary McLeod Bethune, Carter G. Woodson, and Stokely Carmichael were all educational leaders critiqued and criticized by white society for their progressive efforts and initiatives to eradicate economic, political, and educational oppression among African Americans. *Leading While Black: Reflections on the Racial Realities of Black School Leaders Through the Obama Era and Beyond* takes up the complex work of Black leadership for educational equity by using riveting personal narrative to deconstruct inherent tensions and challenges. Floyd Cobb answers important questions such as 'How does the Black experience make our leadership challenges unique?' and 'What are ways to successfully engage in this transformational work in Black bodies that are deliberately and subconsciously profiled in practically every sphere of American life?'. Cobb also presents a framework demonstrating important relationships between equity-mindedness, racial battle fatigue, and racial realism that advances what we know about equity work pathways to naïve hope or committed struggle. This book immediately hooks the reader through personal story, but a complex structural analysis exudes and Cobb ends with inspiration and expectancy for Black leaders in the struggle for educational equity. This book is a must read!"

—Nicole M. Joseph, Teaching and Learning,
Vanderbilt University

"In this extremely important book, Floyd Cobb guides readers through powerful autobiographical accounts of his journey in schools and education. From his early years as a student in mostly White schools to his current role as an educational leader and researcher, readers experience vivid first-person accounts of what it [still] means to live, work, and learn in a society that is far, far from post-racial. With precision and fortitude, Cobb poses and answers a provocative question: What does it mean to lead while Black? Indeed, at a time of serious political, social, economic, and educational uncertainty, Cobb reminds us all that we must study, work to more clearly understand, and situate issues of race, human suffering, and systemic inequity at the very center of our work as those committed to equity in education! If you want to be re-energized to fight for social justice for all students, read this book!"

—H. Richard Milner IV, Helen Faison Endowed Chair of Urban Education,
University of Pittsburgh; Author of *Rac(e)ing to Class*

Leading While Black

BLACK STUDIES & critical thinking

Rochelle Brock and Cynthia Dillard
Executive Editors

Vol. 76

The Black Studies and Critical Thinking series
is part of the Peter Lang Education list.
Every volume is peer reviewed and meets
the highest quality standards for content and production.

PETER LANG
New York • Bern • Frankfurt • Berlin
Brussels • Vienna • Oxford • Warsaw

Floyd Cobb

Leading While Black

Reflections on the Racial Realities of Black School Leaders Through the Obama Era and Beyond

PETER LANG
New York • Bern • Frankfurt • Berlin
Brussels • Vienna • Oxford • Warsaw

Library of Congress Cataloging-in-Publication Data

Names: Cobb, Floyd, author.
Title: Leading while black: reflections on the racial realities of black school leaders
through the Obama era and beyond / Floyd Cobb.
Description: New York: Peter Lang, 2017.
Series: Black studies and critical thinking; vol. 76 | ISSN 1947-5985
Identifiers: LCCN 2017000774 | ISBN 978-1-4331-3444-9 (hardcover: alk. paper)
ISBN 978-1-4331-3443-2 (paperback: alk. paper) | ISBN 978-1-4331-4140-9 (ebook pdf)
ISBN 978-1-4331-4141-6 (epub) | ISBN 978-1-4331-4142-3 (mobi)
Subjects: LCSH: Educational equalization—United States.
Racism in education—United States. | Educational leadership—United States.
African American children—Education. | African American school administrators.
Classification: LCC LC213.2 .C59 2017 | DDC 379.2/6—dc23
LC record available at https://lccn.loc.gov/2017000774
DOI 10.3726/b10905

Bibliographic information published by **Die Deutsche Nationalbibliothek**.
Die Deutsche Nationalbibliothek lists this publication in the "Deutsche
Nationalbibliografie"; detailed bibliographic data are available
on the Internet at http://dnb.d-nb.de/.

The paper in this book meets the guidelines for permanence and durability
of the Committee on Production Guidelines for Book Longevity
of the Council of Library Resources.

Printed in the United States of America

To all of the Black equity minded leaders in the struggle, working to improve the academic experiences for all students.

Contents

Illustrations

Figures

Tables

Prologue

This tribute to my late mentor, John William Buckner, is my attempt to make public many of the lessons he taught me about Black leadership. Buckner was an educational leader who for over thirty years dedicated his life to creating equitable learning environments for students in K–12 schools. High school principal, central office administrator, and Colorado state representative, Buckner was an advocate and role model for many. He was the one many of the administrators of color looked up to and revered for his ability to lead while Black.

I had the privilege of knowing Buckner personally as well as professionally, as he was my father-in-law and, more than that, a "second" father. This is not to suggest that I was lacking in parental guidance; I have two wonderful parents who worked hard and were committed to their children. These exceptional people, while not college graduates, did everything they could to ensure that my sister and I had the experience and educational foundation they lacked. My degrees—two bachelor's, a master's and a Ph.D.—suggest that they succeeded.

However, there were limits to their ability to guide me professionally—a fact not lost on my father, who often told me, "Son, I have taken you as far as I know how. You have exceeded my limits to guide you; from here you are going to have to figure things out on your own." With this in mind, I sought guidance when faced with challenges outside the limits of my parents' expertise: John Buckner was the perfect mentor for me in these situations.

He was there to keep me grounded and help me feel safe as I struggled with the intense vulnerability of trying to live a life that exceeded my parents' greatest hopes. I appreciated his presence because he always helped me feel tethered when I was drifting into the professional sea of uncertainty that every first generation college graduate faces. To lose him far sooner than I expected affected me deeply and ultimately was the final catalyst to the writing of this book.

Now, I do not know if it's normal to live in awe of your father-in-law, but I certainly did. I was utterly astonished at the number of things Buckner was able to accomplish in his time with us. And now more than ever I realize how lucky I was to have, in one person, a father-in-law, mentor, and professional role model. Although I rarely let on, I marveled at how much more he knew than me about everything. Even the one thing that affirmed my expertise in an area—my doctoral thesis—was based on a concept he had discovered at least ten years before me. His depth of knowledge was unmatched and I sought every opportunity to learn from him. I loved to sit and listen to stories about his experiences as a student and as an educator. It was clear that he loved to fight for equality, which meant ensuring that all children received the treatment they deserved.

Buckner and I spent hours discussing educational leadership strategy and the harsh realities of trying to do this job when you are Black. He frequently told me that no matter which role he occupied, there were some who questioned his authority and qualifications simply because he was Black. Nevertheless, Buckner was quick to remind me that our presence in the education system mattered and that we were critical to creating unimagined possibilities for students who looked like us. His philosophy, as revealed in his speech commemorating the anniversary of the Brown vs. Board of Education decision, was simple:

"The faster we can include more people in us and less people in them the quicker we'll make better decisions for all of us."

His advocacy for kids was most obvious during his interactions with the students and community associated with his beloved high school. He was so proud of that school community; it was not only where he worked, but where he lived and chose to educate his children. For him, it was personal. He absolutely loved to brag about his students' countless success stories. When one of his high school graduates would appear on television, Buckner would swell with fatherly pride and say, "You know she went to my school, right?," then relate a short story about that student's success at his school. Then we would talk about other students who went on to great success. He lived to see students succeed and would be the first to correct you if you said anything disparaging about his community.

In a sense, he was the surrogate father of that community. It's understandable: To a generation of families and students he was the only high school principal they knew. He was a constant in an ever-changing world; someone who positively affected countless lives throughout his career.

Buckner touched everyone he met: Students, teachers, counselors, administrators, and support staff. I am proud to say that every week I meet someone who boasts about his effect on their life, whether it's a graduate relating stories about the ways in which he went above and beyond for them or one of his former employees recalling the joy of being hired by and working for him. The stories are endless. John affected more lives than he could possibly know.

John's status as a role model extended far beyond his work with students. This was especially true for Black educators within the district. At a time when professional diversity and Black leadership exemplars in Buckner's school district were sparse, he was a giant. His example was an inspiration to many of us and showed us the type of leader we might one day become. He taught us how to succeed in spite of the challenges inherent in leadership, especially as a person of color. This was true in good times and in bad. He exemplified perseverance when times were hard, when unpopular decisions needed to be made, or in the face of strong disagreement. He taught us to face indignity by standing tall, remaining calm, using our heads, and continuing to advocate for what was right.

I do not know if he fully appreciated the scope of the impact that he had. He was never one to seek the limelight or pursue praise; Buckner's joy derived from seeing the successes of those he supported. A big reason why his loss has been so difficult for me is that he saw in me more than I saw in myself. I think he did that for a lot of people.

Another hero of mine, baseball great Jackie Robinson, once said, "A life is not important except in the impact it has on other lives." Those of us who chose to work in the field of education spend a great deal of our professional lives hoping that, despite the hard work and challenges, we have a significant effect on the lives of our students.

May my father in law John W. Buckner rest in eternal peace knowing that he did just that.

Acknowledgments

When I first sat down to write this book, I was in a considerable amount of pain. Still grieving the passing of my father-in-law and mentor John Buckner and struggling to make sense of a lot that I was observing in the world, I used this work to channel my sorrow and anguish with the hope that it would enable me to find the right words to allow me to make sense of all that I had been feeling. At the completion of this book, I can say that it certainly has and I feel fortunate that I have been blessed with a skill that allowed this.

One of the strange ironies of this process was that I didn't think I had enough words in me to actually sit down and write this book. I knew this work was important but initially thought that it would be best to have it communicated as an edited volume. However, it was a conversation with Rich Milner that convinced me otherwise. Rich gave me the confidence to know that I had the words in me to tell my story as it was definitely one that needed to be told. So first and foremost I want to say thank you to Rich Milner for giving me that final push that I needed to write this book.

Thank you to the scholars who have played such an important role in my life, in my journey to become a writer. To Frank Tuitt, thank you for pushing me to not be scared and to make it a priority to maintain my identity as a scholar-practitioner. Thank you to Nick Cutforth, Bruce Uhrmacher and Maria Salazar for pushing me to become more emotive and descriptive in my writing. Your words were constant reminders as I pushed through this autoethnography. Thank you to Kristina Hesbol for keeping me encouraged and building me up at a time when I needed it most. To Nicole Joseph, "my sistah" you are awesome. You exude joy and are such an outstanding person. You have made me a better scholar even though my primary role is that of a practitioner. Every time I sit down and write, you remind me that you achieved your goal to keep me writing. I would like to send a special thank you to Laura Meyer for your support in the editing process. Having your perspective on this was needed and I thank you for your honest feedback. A special thank you goes out to Donna Ford and everyone in the Race mentoring group. Being a part of that network reminded me of the importance of my voice and its need to be used. Finally, I would like to thank Gloria Ladson-Billings and Margaret Beale Spencer for your mentorship at AERA on understanding what it took to get published. It brought me such joy to see your excitement when I let you know that I got a contract. Please know that this effort could not have been possible without your support.

Next, I need to say thank you to the group of individuals that I have leaned on the most throughout this process. To Mary Johnson and Elliott Asp, thank you both for being such incredible advisors and friends. You are both such incredible souls. Thank you for always finding a way to build me up in a world that was relentless in trying to tear me down. To Sarah Bridich, thank you for being one of my early readers and thank you for your incredible friendship throughout the years. You are one of the most purely genuine people that I have ever had the privilege of knowing. You're always there, and I can always count you to give me honest feedback in love. I am fortunate to have you as a friend in my life. To Scott and Dayna, thank you for being such incredible friends as I've struggled through this writing process.

I cannot adequately express how much I appreciate you. You two are always there, always. That's true friendship. Thank you.

Finally, I would like to say thank you to my family. To my parents, Floyd and Ozell thank you for instilling me with resilience. There have been a number of times where I questioned whether I could move forward and whenever I would get to that point I would always think of you. You two have set me up so well and I live everyday to make you proud. To Ma'am Janet Buckner, thank you for being the mentor that I needed in John's absence. You are absolutely wonderful. You exude love. Thank you for always seeing me as your son. To Sydney and Ashlyn, thank you for giving Daddy time to write this book. I finally finished the book with all those words Sydney. Hopefully when you're older and you get a chance to read it, it can be something that will make you proud of your Dad. Finally, to my wife Jennifer, I love you. Thank you for letting me be me, and thank you for always being willing to encourage me as I think about pursuing another adventure. Most importantly thank you for always seeing me the way I want to be seen. I am so lucky to have you as my wife!

Preface

If there's a book that you want to read, but it hasn't been written yet, then you must write it.

—*Toni Morrison*

Firsts and Only's

For most of my life, I have been fascinated by Black Americans who were either the first or the only to accomplish something. Whether that was Jackie Robinson, Thurgood Marshall, Tom Bradley, Althea Gibson, Colin Powell, or Barack Obama, I have always had a deep reverence for the resilience, courage, and intestinal fortitude it takes to live as the example for others. I'm sure part of my fascination with these and other individuals has a lot to do with the fact that I have spent the greater part of my life being a first and only. Certainly, not to the scale and magnitude of those mentioned above, but I am nonetheless intimately familiar with the weight of the burden and perseverance necessary to carry the hopes and aspirations of those like me.

For me, the reality of this weight became self-evident in my youth. As one of the few Black children in my suburban San Diego neighborhood and almost always the *only* Black student in each of my classrooms, I became accustomed to what it meant to be a living example of one's race at an early age. Never having the advantage of blending in or the privilege of being seen for my individuality, I have almost always known the responsibility that "only-ness" can bring. I often felt that I had to be perfect, knowing that the decisions I made and actions I took would affect every individual who followed me. Because of this, I've always felt a fictive kinship with Black Americans who have had to occupy this space, no matter who they were.

This feeling started in elementary school when I developed an admiration for Jackie Robinson. I came to know the historical figure through a children's book titled, *The Value of Courage: The Story of Jackie Robinson* (Johnson, 1977). The book described Robinson's life from childhood through retirement, focusing on his courage at not lashing out in the face of unprecedented discrimination. Using a mythical rag baseball to represent his inner voice, the story details Robinson's emotional struggles with the unfairness of racial prejudice.

The story detailed the countless examples of discrimination that Robinson faced and how each hurt him deeply, inspiring him to fight back and at other times to give up due to the injustice. Nonetheless, despite the incredible pain that each of these incidents caused, Robinson found a way to resist his temptations because of an inner voice that reminded him of the example that he set for those who followed. The mythical rag told him, "Having courage means seeing things through. No matter how hard it is, you've got to keep trying" (Johnson, p. 47).

As a child who never truly saw my identity reflected in the curriculum, Robinson became my exemplar. While I in no way experienced the depths of discrimination that he faced while desegregating major league baseball, his story nonetheless sustained me through my hard times. Whenever I was teased for being different or called a nigger on the playground, it was his story of courage that helped me to understand which fights to wage and the way to go about it. Despite my loneliness at school, his story reminded me that I was not alone when

I had negative experiences associated with my race. This book was my saving grace.

To be honest, at such a young age, I am not sure whether I understood all the words in the sixty-three-page book, but I know for certain that I was able to understand the message. This biography was the only book I had ever read that expressed my emotions around being "the only." Whenever I checked it out from my elementary school library (which was often), I would thumb through the pages and carefully study the illustrations about the Black baseball player from California who, just like me, struggled with feelings of being all alone.

I looked to this book for comfort and lessons from Robinson. However, as with all things in our youth, there came a point where the words on that children's book simply were not enough. As I matured, the race realities of being "the only" became more nuanced and complex than the phrases from an illustrated book. In a strange way, I have been on a quest to find those words ever since. This book is my attempt to use the words that I have found to describe the consequential feeling of living a life as the first and/or only.

Why This Book?

As I reach the mid-way point of my career as an educational leader, I feel that I've finally found a way to bring words to a question that has plagued me for a very long time. The question is as specific as it is provocative, and is revealed to be incredibly complex when the layers that surround it are peeled back. It is one that left me unsettled for the entirety of my young career and gnawed at me for most of my life. That question is: What does it mean to lead while Black?

In answering this question, I have chosen to narrow my focus to leaders committed to improving the academic experiences of Black children in suburban educational contexts, because these individuals must do their work while negotiating the burden of being the first or the only. This is not to suggest that Black leaders in urban environments have an easier path or cannot relate to my experiences, because recent studies have demonstrated that Black educators from across the nation experience a racial burden independent of the educational context (Bailey, 2016; Griffin & Takie, 2016). Nonetheless, the racial visibility and vulnerability that Black leaders in suburban environments encounter is unique. Therefore, my aim in focusing on suburban educational environments is not only to reflect this reality but also my experiences.

In writing about what it means to lead while Black, it is important to note that I am looking to describe and not prescribe. Therefore, I want to be clear that this is not a "how-to" book. There is no checklist of actions to perform; that work can never exist. Moreover, my goal in this book is not to blame or shame but to prepare emerging and aspiring Black leaders for the unique burdens we can face. Therefore, this work ultimately is about reality as I have come to understand it. More importantly, it seeks to reveal how the Black racial identity is confronted with unique challenges when attempting to bring about transformational change in our schools. In this work, I try to explain how we negotiate the invisible tax (King, 2016) that is placed upon us (by people of all races) in our efforts to bring about change in a field whose actions do not always align with its stated intentions.

Specifically, this book reflects how equity-minded Black leaders can be reflexively perceived and treated, thus directly influencing how we go about our work. Drawing from lessons passed down to me by my late father-in-law and mentor, John Buckner, this book is my professional narrative ascent (Stepo, 1991). Using the period of the Obama presidency as the backdrop for this work, I reveal how I begrudgingly came to accept the racial realities of my leadership identity and how my efforts to bring about change and improve the academic experience of children who look like me is never race-neutral.

At its core, this book is about my acknowledgment and reluctant acceptance of the inherent social vulnerability of equity-minded Black educational leaders in suburban contexts. The word *vulnerable* reveals my focus on how we are capable of being wounded or open to assault in our efforts to support the achievement of students who look like us (Turner, 2006). Therefore, it is not my aim to have my readers pity those of us who make the decision to engage in the fight for equity; rather, it is my attempt to express the unique ways that we are capable of being wounded or open to assault in our efforts to bring about change. More than that, I have tried to describe how we must contend with uncertainty, risk, and emotional exposure (Brown, 2012) when doing our work as, most likely, the first or only.

Acceptance of my racialized social vulnerability in educational leadership has taken me an incredible amount of time to accept, as I have taken every measure possible to avoid it. Nonetheless, I have found a way to persevere, live more freely, and lead in ways that keep me from avoiding despair. I have learned that the very things that make me the most vulnerable also serve as the source of my greatest strength (Lorde, 2012).

Therefore, I have written this book to support aspiring and emerging Black educational leaders who might be contending with the same questions of how it can feel to lead while Black. Specifically, I am writing to those who are deeply committed to using their roles as professionals to continue the fight against educational inequality. By focusing this book on the experience of Black leaders, I do not suggest that other equity-minded leaders who have marginalized identities are less susceptible to harm, because change leadership is hard and dangerous work (Heifietz & Linsky, 2002) for everyone. Instead, this work is an opportunity to speak specifically to Black leaders to illuminate a perspective and bring voice to an experience that is rarely shared. It is my hope that readers can make meaning from my experiences and learn lessons to apply to their own as they fight to correct the unequal conditions of underserved children in our nation's public schools.

The idea for this book emerged over several years but truly became solidified when I attended the National Alliance of Black School Educators Conference in 2015. It was here that I gave my first presentation on this topic in a conference strand that was specifically focused on Black leaders who work in non-Black settings. Not yet confident that this concept was worthy of an entire book, I took this opportunity to first share my ideas with a like-minded audience in hopes that I might solicit some feedback on what, at the time, were some very rough thoughts.

I remember being uncharacteristically nervous prior to this presentation. Normally I am at home in front of a large audience, as I have given countless presentations and speeches at conferences all across the country. However, this one was different because, unlike my other presentations, it was personal. I knew that in exposing the pain of my reality I was taking an emotional risk and, while highly unlikely, I had a hard time shaking the fear that this reality would be mine alone.

As the room filled for the ninety-minute session, I walked around to calm myself. Although I knew the room was going to be safe, I could only think of the worst. This presentation was not just about data or research—it was about me. I was the subject of study. As much as I wanted this presentation to go well and reflect the effort and energy I put into it, more than that I wanted confirmation that my experiences, although distinct, were not singular. As the time drew near for the presentation to begin, I took a deep breath before turning down the volume on Aretha Franklin's version of *Young, Gifted and Black* and started the presentation.

After presenting just a few slides, I realized that I was not alone in my experience. The Black educational leaders who filled the room and held various positions across the country were just like me, struggling to make sense of this thing we call leadership. While we were in different cities, had different roles, and differing amounts of professional experience, the weight we carried and the burdens we felt were so universal that my story could have been any one of theirs.

I was overwhelmed by the response at the end of my presentation because, as I was told by many of the attendees, this was the first time that someone named how they felt. Through that presentation, I signaled that I could see their authentic self, thereby giving them the very thing I was hoping to receive because of my attendance at the conference. Those responses indicated how rarely our stories get told and helped me decide that I needed to write this book. With this experience in mind, *Leading While Black* was born.

Scholarly Approach

I come to this work as a scholar-practitioner. Tenkasi and Hay regarded these individuals "as actors who have one foot each in the worlds of academia and practice and are pointedly interested in advancing the causes of both theory and practice" (2008, p. 49). Specifically, a scholar-practitioner is a "professional who knows how to abstract new knowledge from experiences in organizations" (Wasserman & Kram, 2009, p. 19). In our work, we use our dual identities to draw "from diverse conceptual, theoretical, philosophical, and methodological tools to create a bricolage of scholarly practice, shaping one's identity and at the same time working to enable 'Others' to develop identities" (Jenlink, 2003, pp. 5–6). As scholar practitioners, we have professional identities that are dynamic. We are regarded as both thinkers and doers (Kram, Wasserman, & Yip, 2012) who rely on our scholarly foundation to address the practical issues that confront us daily. We use our knowledge *of* practice to apply knowledge *in* practice (Hampton, 2010).

I have chosen to reveal my scholar-practitioner perspective using critical autoethnography, a qualitative autobiographical genre that allows the researcher to examine "the self in institutional and professional contexts with an eye not only toward a better understanding of ourselves as anthropologists, but also a more vigorous reflection on the institutional practices and fields in which we operate" (Tilley-Lubbs, 2014, p. 269). Autoethnography is a form of "research and writing that seeks to describe and systematically analyze (graphy) personal experience (auto) in order to understand cultural experience (ethno)" (Ellis, Adams, & Bochner, 2011). Adams, Holman-Jones, and Ellis contended that "[w]hen we do autoethnography, we look inward into our identities, thoughts, feelings, and experiences, and outward into our relationships, communities, and cultures" (2015, p. 46). Through the performance of autoethnography, the researcher remains the focus of the study and becomes "the epistemological and ontological nexus upon which the research process turns" (Spry, 2001, p. 711). In performing this method, the researcher tries to "inspire readers to reflect critically upon their own life experience, their constructions of self, and their interactions with others within sociohistorical contexts" (p. 711) and to take action.

Autoethnographers make use of personal experience to expose the "vulnerable self" (Patton, 2002, p. 85) and demonstrate how one's lived experience can offer "insights into the larger culture or subculture of which you are a part" (p. 86). Therefore, we rely upon personal memories and self-reflective experiences as our data sources, understanding that the data we select are subject to our interpretation (Chang, 2008). Consequently, autoethnography allows the reader to understand how the researcher's "self-conception profoundly influences [his] cognitions, emotions, and interactions" (Ting Toomey, 1999, p. 27 as cited in Waymer, 2008).

Critical autoethnography encourages readers to see "people in the process of figuring out what to do, how to live, and the meaning of their struggles" (Adams, Holman-Jones, & Ellis, p. 130). Appropriately, autoethnography is regarded as a suitable method for revealing one's experience with injustice, because personal experience can "make the case for cultural change, but also embod[y] the change it calls into being" (Adams, Holman-Jones & Ellis, pp. 113–114).

Those who know me will likely be surprised by my choice of methodology because I am regarded as a notoriously private person. I am a self-professed introvert who shares very little about himself and finds emotional safety in solitude. I am most comfortable when I am alone. I have likely done so to not feel more vulnerable than necessary because, when living a life while Black, vulnerability can feel omnipresent. However, the experiences and emotions that led to the creation of this book forced me to push that instinct aside, take a risk, and step outside of myself out of a sense of obligation to young and emerging Black leaders who are hoping to make sense of equity leadership. I took a chance with my vulnerability and wrote this book to let them know that they are not alone.

Critical Race Theory

Given this book's title, I have obviously chosen to make race a central theme of this work and have chosen to use critical race theory in education as my interpretive lens for this autoethnography.

Critical race theory is a movement that started in the field of law with the assemblage of "a collection of activists and scholars interested in studying and transforming the relationship between race, racism and power" (Delgado & Stefancic, 2001, p. 2). Emerging in the mid-1970s from the work of the movement's patriarchs, Derrick Bell and Alan Freeman, critical race theory reflected legal scholars' ongoing frustration with the pace of racial reform. Thus, critical race theorists used their scholarship to critique the perceived objectivity and neutrality of the law by highlighting its repeated detrimental effects on racially minoritized individuals (Ladson-Billings, 1998).

In enacting this scholarship, critical race theorists rely on fundamental principles called tenets. While they are not considered doctrine due to disagreement among members of the community who apply this theory (Delgado & Stefancic, 2001), critical race theorists *do* agree on the basic proposition that the socially constructed idea of race is a foundational component of American life that confers status. Critical race theorists assert that race has historically been used in conjunction with the law to bestow advantages and disadvantages to members within socially constructed groups, leading to contemporary, normalized assumptions about the social order.

Consequently, critical race theorists use scholarship to challenge that normative structure by centering race and utilizing the experiential knowledge of people of color to name their own reality (Delgado, 1989; Delgado & Stefancic, 2001; Matsuda et al., 1993) and disrupt that normativity. Critical race theorists "emphasize our marginality and try to turn it toward advantageous perspective building and concrete advocacy of those oppressed by race, and other interlocking factors of gender, economic class, and sexual orientation" (Delgado & Stefancic,

2005, p. 79). Critical race theory writings prioritize storytelling and counter-storytelling methods to not only challenge the neutrality of the law but also to "communicate understanding and reassurance to needy souls trapped in a hostile world" (Bell, Stefancic & Delgado, 2005, p. 82).

While critical race theory started as a legal movement, its application to the field of education is evident because public education is a direct by-product of laws enacted by politicians. As Ladson-Billings (1998) noted, "States generate legislation and enact laws designed to proscribe the contours of education" (p. 17), thus making critical race theory a natural fit when examining the racial complexities of public schools. Among the aforementioned principles, critical race theory in education interrogates the racial effect of macro-level policies and micro-level practices in schools (Zamidio, Russell, Rios, & Bridgeman, 2011). Whether it is through curriculum, instruction, funding, assessment, teacher evaluation, or student discipline, critical race theory illuminates the racial implications of actions that can at times be regarded as neutral.

Organization of the Book

I begin Chapter 1 by detailing a few of my "critical moments in post-racial(?) America." Delgado and Stefancic argued that "critical moments" are events and inflection points that are "…easy to discern in retrospect" (2013, p. 24) but less so at the time they occur. For these moments to be fully appreciated, greater knowledge and context are required. The critical moments in the first chapter center on my pivotal conversation about education leadership with my mentor and father-in-law, John Buckner. The conversation occurred on the precipice of the 2009 election of Barack Obama and I, like many, was hopeful (emphasis added) that the positive sentiments elicited from his campaign would transfer to Black leaders more broadly. After experiencing the positivity of the Obama campaign, I was optimistic that other Black leaders and, quite possibly, Black people in general would also be seen in a similar light. However, it was not long into the administration of our nation's first

Black President that my hopes were shattered, forcing me to question what it meant to lead while Black.

Foregrounding this chapter in postracial ideology (Cho, 2009), I build on the work of numerous scholars (Andrews & Tuitt, 2013; Cho, 2008; Crenshaw, 2010; Fasching-Varner, Albert, Mitchell, & Allen, 2015; Warren, 2012), who challenge the concept of post-racialism as a myth. I will explain its nuances and the ways in which it is applied by detailing my experience with the President's first, oddly controversial back-to-school speech and my frustrated efforts to close the achievement/opportunity gap. I close the chapter by reflecting upon my experiences, the broader context of post-racialism, and what it means to equity-minded Black leadership.

The second chapter details my double consciousness as a school leader who has had to negotiate the tension between feeling coerced into behaving in the passive ways that my colleagues wish and being an unapologetically Black leader for equity who quickly addresses institutionalized discrimination in all of its forms. Using my professional and undergraduate experiences as the backdrop for this chapter, I illuminate how racial discrimination is performed through the practice of humiliation and how the normalization of that behavior historically and contemporarily defines what it means to be Black. The chapter provides examples of how perceptions of Black Americans, particularly Black students, are supported by long-held stereotypes born out of the minstrelsy, complicating efforts to address inequities in schools. This section concludes with a narrative about my sense-making of my double consciousness and the impact it has had on my role as a professional.

The third chapter extends the theme of double consciousness by illuminating the psychological toll that Black Americans experience as we ascend to professional roles that lay outside of the stereotypical norm. Relating this phenomenon to racial profiling, I reveal how the normalized practices of humiliation and bullying merge in society and the workplace to coerce Black Americans to behave in racially palatable (Carbado, 2016) ways. Throughout this chapter, I reveal how these practices were applied to our nation's first Black President, leading to my acceptance of what it means to lead while Black.

The fourth chapter focuses on how I have made sense of my reality. I offer a detailed explanation of my theoretical framework, Leading While Black (see theoretical framework below). This chapter focuses heavily on research that supports the theoretical frame, including of equity-mindedness (Bensimon, 2005), racial battle fatigue (Smith 2004; Smith, Allen, & Danley, 2007), and racial realism (Bell, Delgado, & Stefancic, 2005). The Center for Urban Education at the University of Southern California's website defines equity-mindedness as "a demonstrated awareness of and willingness to address equity issues among institutional leaders and staff." The concept of racial battle fatigue "addresses the physiological and psychological strain exacted on racially marginalized groups and the amount of energy lost dedicated to coping with racial microaggressions and racism" (Smith, Allen, & Danley, 2007, p. 555). Finally, racial realism is a mindset that acknowledges the subordinated status of Black Americans despite some advances. The acceptance of this theory allows for the "creation and activation of racial strategies that can bring fulfillment and even triumph" (Bell, Delgado, & Stefancic, 2005, p. 85). Collectively, they create the broader theoretical framework of Leading While Black. This framework will be used as a foundation for grounding the narratives of equity-minded Black educational leaders in the postracial context.

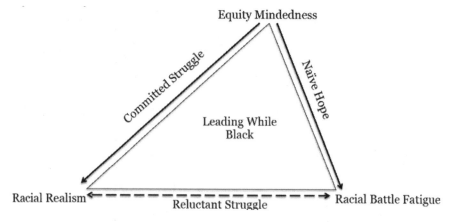

Figure P.1—Leading While Black Theoretical Framework.

The fifth and final chapter of the book concludes with my reflections on what I learned about leadership during the Obama era. This section highlights the importance of similarly situated Black leaders in this moment and concludes with a call to avoid despair, noting that there is meaning in our struggle.

A Final Word

When I began the process of composing this book during the 2016 presidential campaign, I was convinced that Americans were experiencing another historical moment, one in which our nation would once again be led by an individual whose identity was that of a first or an only. While I am a realist when it comes to progress toward equality in our country, I assumed that after having a remarkable Black man lead our country for the prior eight years, the United States was ready for an imminently qualified woman (despite her many political controversies) to take the reins. Considering the choice of presidential candidates, their depth of knowledge on major issues and, most importantly, the reprehensible behavior repeatedly displayed by the Republican candidate, it seemed obvious to me that we would end one historic era by commencing upon another. Ultimately, of course, I was surprised and disappointed (like many others) to learn that my prediction did not come true, leaving me with questions about where we are as a country and, more importantly, about our willingness to be led by those who do not fall into a stereotypical mold.

The fact that I was in the process of putting the finishing touches on this work at the time of this decision led me to question the impact that this broader national decision would have on this book. However, after discussing this with a close friend and taking a step back from my efforts, it became clear to me that, despite my surprise, the 2016 presidential election touched upon what I had hoped to write about all along: Leadership for equity is a struggle. Just when we think we are close to achieving it, we lift our heads up and realize how much further we have to go.

References

Adams, T. E., Holman-Jones, S., & Ellis, C. (2015). *Autoethnography: Understanding qualitative research*. New York, NY: Oxford University Press.

Bailey, S. (2016). An examination of student and educator experiences in Denver public schools through the voices of African-American teachers and administrators. Retrieved from http://www.documentcloud.org/documents/3006020-Bailey-Final-Report.html#document/p1

Bell, D. A., Delgado, R., & Stefancic, J. (2005). *The Derrick Bell reader*. New York, NY: NYU Press.

Bensimon, E. M. (2005). Closing the achievement gap in higher education: An organizational learning perspective. *New Directions for Higher Education, 131,* 99.

Carbado, D. (2016) Critical what what? In G. Ladson-Billings & W. Tate (Eds.). *Covenant keepers: Derrick Bell's enduring education legacy* (pp. vii–xxii). New York, NY: Peter Lang.

Chang, H. (2008). *Autoethnography as method* (Vol. 1). Walnut Creek, CA: Left Coast Press.

Crenshaw, K. W. (2010). Twenty years of critical race theory: Looking back to move forward. *Connecticut Law Review, 43,* 1253.

Cho, S. (2008). Post-racialism. *Iowa Law Review, 94,* 1589.

Delgado, R., & Stefancic, J., (2013) Discerning critical moments. In Lynn, M., & Dixson, A. D. (Eds.). *Handbook of critical race theory in education* (pp. 23–33). New York, NY: Routledge.

Dumas, M. J. (2014). "Losing an arm": Schooling as a site of black suffering. *Race, Ethnicity and Education, 17*(1), 1–29.

Ellis, C., Adams, T. & Bochner, A. (2011). *Autoethnography: An overview*. Forum: Qualitative Social Research. Retrieved from http://www.qualitative-research.net/index.php/fqs/article/view/1589/3096

Griffin, A., & Takie, H., (2016). *Through our eyes: Perspective and reflections from Black teachers*. Research Report. Washington, DC: Education Trust.

Hampton, K. (2010). Transforming School and Society: Examining the theoretical foundations of scholar-practitioner leadership. *Scholar-Practitioner Quarterly, 4*(2), 185–193.

Heifetz, R. A., & Linsky, M. (2002). *Leadership on the line*. Cambridge, MA: Harvard Business Review Press.

Hochschild, A. R. (2012). *The managed heart: Commercialization of human feeling*. Berkeley, CA: University of California Press.

Jenlink, P. (2003). Identity and culture work: The scholar-practitioner as public intellectual. *Scholar-Practitioner Quarterly: A Journal for the Scholar-Practitioner Leader, 1*(4), 3–8.

Johnson, S. (1977). *The value of courage: The story of Jackie Robinson*. La Jolla, CA: Value Tales Publishing.

King, J. (2016, May 15). The invisible tax on teachers of color. *Washington Post.* Retrieved from https://www.washingtonpost.com/opinions/the-invisible-tax-on-black-teachers/2016/05/15/6b7bea06-16f7-11e6-aa55-670cabef46e0_story.html?utm_term=.56d0903eff50

Ladson-Billings, G. (1998). Just what is critical race theory and what's it doing in a nice field like education? *International Journal of Qualitative Studies in Education, 11*(1), 7–24.

Lorde, A. (2012). *Sister outsider: Essays and speeches.* New York, NY: Crossing Press.

Kram, K. E., Wasserman, I. C., & Yip, J. (2012). Metaphors of identity and professional practice: Learning from the scholar-practitioner. *The Journal of Applied Behavioral Science 48(3),* 304-341.

Matsuda, M., Lawrence, C., Delgado, R. & Crenshaw, K. (Eds.) (1993). *Words that wound: Critical race theory, assaultive speech and the first amendment.* Boulder, CO: Westview Press.

Sleeter, C. E. (2001). Preparing teachers for culturally diverse schools research and the overwhelming presence of whiteness. *Journal of Teacher Education, 52*(2), 94–106.

Smedley, A., & Smedley, B. D. (2005). Race as biology is fiction, racism as a social problem is real: Anthropological and historical perspectives on the social construction of race. *American Psychologist, 60*(1), 16.

Stepto R. (1991). *From behind the veil.* Chicago, IL: University of Illinois Press.

Tenkasi, R. V., & Hay, G. W. (2008). Following the second legacy of Aristotle: The scholar-practitioner as an epistemic technician. In A. B. Shani, S. A. Mohrman, W. A. Pasmore, B. N. Stymne, & N. Adler (Eds.). *Handbook of collaborative management research* (pp. 49–72). Thousand Oaks, CA: Sage.

Tilley-Lubbs, G. A. (2014). Critical autoethnography and the vulnerable self as researcher. *Multidisciplinary Journal of Educational Research, 4*(3), 268–285.

Turner, B. (2006). *Vulnerability and human rights.* State College, PA. Pennsylvania State University Press.

Warren, C. A. (2012). The effect of post-racial theory on education. *Journal for Critical Education Policy Studies, 10*(1), 197–216.

Wasserman, I. C., & Kram, K. E. (2009). Enacting the scholar-practitioner role: An exploration of narratives. *The Journal of Applied Behavioral Science, 45*(1), 12–38.

Waymer, D. (2008). A man: An autoethnographic analysis of Black male identity negotiation. *Qualitative Inquiry, 14*(6), 968–989.

Chapter 1

Critical Moments in Postracial America

For, while the tale of how we suffer, and how we are delighted and how we may triumph is never new, it always must be heard. There isn't any other tale to tell, it's the only light we've got in all this darkness.

—*James Baldwin, Sonny's Blues, 1957*

Post-Racial Realism

Whenever I engage in conversations about educational leadership with emerging school leaders who are also Black, the first thing that comes to mind is my late father-in-law, John Buckner. Buckner was a mentor, someone I placed on a pedestal because he was a living example of everything I hoped to be. He was a kind man who had a beautiful family and was highly respected in the community, a sharp dresser, highly intellectual, and incredibly principled. He knew who he was and the things in which he believed, making it obvious to anyone he met that he was comfortable in his own skin.

Despite being my father-in-law, I held Buckner in such high regard that I never felt fully comfortable referring to him by his first name. As clinical as it might sound to some, I regarded the title of "father-in-law" as a term of endearment because he was a father figure in a way not too different from my birth father, whom I also love dearly. He was just that special to me and, as someone who pursued a career in the same school district in which he was employed, I stood proudly on his shoulders, making it my mission to never let him down.

One of the things I've missed the most since Buckner's passing is our countless conversations about educational leadership. Education was his life and a topic he cared about deeply. As someone who had as many years of practice in school leadership as I have had years alive, he had a wealth of knowledge about the field. I was always grateful for his willingness to share his numerous stories, his experiences, and his lessons with me.

As a Black man in a leadership role in a suburban Colorado school district—the same district where I held the same role, albeit years after him—he had a unique set of experiences and stories that were specific to his lived identity. I treasured the opportunities to apply what I'd learned from him to similar problems. As a mentor, he was careful to guide me without being overbearing. He encouraged and supported me, but gave me enough space to find my own way. In giving advice he was always careful to let me know what he thought, without spending a great deal of time trying to convince me that I should do what he said. He would nudge instead of pull. He would guide instead of force, knowing that if I did not take his advice in the moment, I would eventually come to understand what he was trying to say. He knew that this was necessary for my professional and personal growth, so that I could have ownership of arriving at that understanding through my experience.

Buckner saw his presence as a leader in a suburban school system as central to the fight to end racial inequality. Simply put, it was his moral imperative. Specifically, he was fixated and incredibly frustrated with the persistent underperformance of Black children in our school classrooms, particularly on standardized exams. To him, the disparity just did not make sense and, as a matter of fact, should not exist. As a Black man who experienced academic success in his youth, he was unwilling to believe that Black children were inherently less intelligent or somehow incapable of performing well on standardized exams. "The children are fine," he would say, "so we can't blame them for the academic situations in which we put them."

Buckner believed deeply in the business maxim that "all organizations are perfectly designed to get the results that they get" (Hanna, 1998, p. 36) and consequently he was confident that educators could find the solution to system-wide inequities simply by interrogating decisions made within the organization. He believed that racial performance disparities had everything to do with how children were treated by schools in relation to their access to advanced coursework and, subsequently, could be corrected if schools adjusted their academic treatment of Black children. He frequently expressed to me his belief that the achievement gap was simply a result of different learning experiences for Black students. Thus, the issue of unequal performance could be resolved if more Black students were given greater access to college preparatory courses. To him, the solution to the achievement gap was no more complicated than this and, as a principal for seventeen years; he made it his career goal to address that central problem.

Early in my career, whenever we discussed the achievement gap, I would politely and respectfully hear him out and think to myself that the solution that he offered to such a complex phenomenon sounded too simple to be true. In spite of my limited experience, I was convinced he was wrong. To put it bluntly, I thought the old man was crazy. From my perspective, academic experiences were irrelevant when compared to the other factors that are commonly associated with the achievement gap such as teacher belief systems and the instructional practices that manifest as a result. While I agreed with him that the cause of test score inequality did not rest with the children themselves, I was convinced that the problem had more to do with bias in the exams and culturally insensitive instruction leading me to believe that we should focus our efforts here. These reasons were far more complex and sounded much more plausible than the rationale he offered. While the issue of unequal access to college preparatory experiences never occurred to me, I nonetheless assumed that the courses in which students were enrolled were appropriate and had *nothing* to do with how students performed on standardized exams.

Further entrenching my belief that he must be mistaken was his lack of success in solving the problem in his school. Considering that, his solution had such a simple premise, it seemed obvious to me that as a building principal he could have addressed it, yet he had not. As the one in charge of the school, it seemed apparent to me that he had the authority to make any initiative a reality. Because he was the building principal, he was in charge and could set the tone and direction of his building, creating systems and structures to address the inequities that pained him so greatly. If his idea of greater access to college preparatory coursework was so solid, then why as a principal was he unable to make it a reality? There had to be something else.

Although my confusion about his lack of success concerned me, my immense respect for him prevented me from pushing the issue. Therefore, a number of times when we discussed the achievement gap (which was often), I would smile and politely nod, wondering what I was missing. I knew he was capable, I knew he understood how to manage change, and I knew he had done his research. Nonetheless, I struggled to understand how someone who was so intelligent and had such professional authority could not bring his idea of increasing access to rigorous coursework to fruition. This just did not make sense to me: shouldn't this have been easy for him? I knew he had the skills and knowledge but for some reason he could not seem to make it work. There was something that I had to be missing.

This pattern seemed to repeat itself often until one day, sitting in his kitchen; I summoned enough courage to inquire about what it was that I did not understand. I will never forget his surprising answer: "Floyd, what you will find throughout your career is that there are some people out there, regardless of race, who have a hard time being led by a Black person." He continued, "It doesn't matter what race they are (Black, White, Asian, you name it), some people just have a hard time taking direction from a Black person, especially when it comes to those who want to improve the lives of Black children." He went on to describe the many times his dignity had been assaulted, the facts he presented challenged, and his authority dismissed by those who reported to him. He talked about the subversion he faced and the sabotage he encountered in ways that he felt his White peers did not. From his perspective, the fact that he was a highly experienced building principal with a strong academic background did not matter as much as the fact that he was Black. Race could not be transcended. Concluding his reflections, he stated, "I know this is unfair but that's just the reality of Black leadership. This is my reality, it's that of others and it will likely be yours, so know that and find a way to succeed anyway. You're smart enough to do it."

Quite naturally, I felt a sense of disbelief when he told me this. However, more than that I was hurt. I assumed that once one attained a leadership position that race remained minimal relative to the authority that one's title offered. Therefore, it was impossible to conceive that someone with his background, credentials, relationships and, most importantly, expertise could be disregarded simply because he was Black. There was just no way that this could be—I was convinced there must have been something that he was not telling me. Had he simply grown weary at the end of his career? Was he frustrated at the magnitude of a few decisions he wished he could take back? Did his words indicate nothing more than regret? What was it?

Despite his words of caution, I struggled with what he was telling me but once again out of an abundance of respect for my father-in-law and mentor, I decided not to pursue it further even though his response left me yearning for more. There was something that I could see about this reflection that was deeply personal. Therefore, despite my many questions, I decided it was best to not push the issue, even though not getting answers to them would leave me feeling unsettled.

Nonetheless, despite my bewilderment toward his response, I believed that what he told me about Black leadership, much like the achievement gap before that was wrong. I viewed what he was saying as nothing more than an oversimplification of a few isolated experiences he encountered and I thought it was presumptuous of him to generalize his experience to other Black leaders. In my heart, I knew he was mistaken and that it was possible for Black leaders to be respected in a way that he never experienced and that ultimately race could be transcended. However, more than that, I did not want to take into account what he just told me because I did not like the way his response made me feel. Accepting his premise would leave me hopeless and crush the optimism I had for what was possible in my burgeoning career. Therefore, for my own sake of idealism and hope for my future, I needed him to be wrong.

Consequently, I started to rationalize to myself why I thought his ideas were adrift. I knew that my path would be different because unlike him, I had a mentor who had countless years of experience to help guide me whenever it was needed. Therefore, I knew that even if the things he told me were true, that I could rely on his advice, combined with my smarts to overcome any trials I faced. I was convinced that I could succeed where he had not because I was entering into school leadership at a time that was much more progressive than when he worked and I was going to find a way to prove to him that his prior statements about Black leaders were wrong.

One of the ways I looked to prove my point was through the example of Barack Obama. From the moment I watched Obama give his keynote address at the 2004 Democratic National Convention I knew he was special. As the multiracial son of an immigrant father, he encapsulated the possibilities of what could be accomplished in this country. His unifying message was about hope, and his dynamic presence and rhetorical genius reminded us of the greatness of America and the possibilities she offers.

> Do we participate in a politics of cynicism, or do we participate in a politics of hope? I'm not talking about blind optimism here, the almost willful ignorance that thinks unemployment will go away if we just don't think about it, or health care crisis will solve itself if we just ignore it. That's not what I'm talking about(?). I'm talking about something more substantial. It's the hope of slaves sitting around a fire singing freedom songs; the hope of immigrants setting out for distant shores; the hope of a young naval lieutenant bravely patrolling the Mekong Delta; the hope of a millworker's son who dares to defy the odds; the hope of a skinny kid with a funny name who believes that

America has a place for him, too. Hope in the face of difficulty, hope in the face of uncertainty, the audacity of hope: In the end, that is God's greatest gift to us, the bedrock of this nation, a belief in things not seen, a belief that there are better days ahead. (Obama, 2004)

In Barack Obama, I saw a leader who offered a vision of our country in which everyone could take part. While he was not an educator, the leadership parallels were still easy to draw as he presented new possibilities that I had never imagined. In him, I saw a Black leader who was unafraid to address the realities of race while not getting so caught up in the slow pace of change that he sent a message of despair. His words painted a beautiful picture of what was possible and made everyone believe that they had a responsibility to play their part in making this country a better place for everyone.

One of the things I appreciated most about Obama was the fact that he was relatable, allowing me to see myself in him. He knew my experience and understood the challenges that Black males in this country face and, most importantly, was not afraid to talk about it. In Obama, I saw a man capable of ignoring the race-based negativity thrown at him while openly discussing the adverse assumptions that come with being a Black male. Obama was different: he leaned in where others routinely leaned back, walked with a swagger, wore nice suits, epitomized cool, and controlled the way he wanted the world to see him and not the other way around. He was so unique, in fact, that many wondered whether he was "Black enough." Highly intellectual, charismatic, and a master of oratory, Barack Obama was a once-in-a-generation leader who displayed talents the likes of which the country had never seen.

Obama was masterful at navigating the nearly impossible terrain of politics and race. Where, in the past, successful Black politicians did everything they could to minimize the historic significance of race in this country, Obama embraced it. Illustrated brilliantly in his historic speech "A More Perfect Union," Obama was able use his multiracial background and his oratorical expertise to present the historical realities of both Black and White America, creating an opportunity for both perspectives to be heard in a way that no other politician had. He found a way to give voice to those in suffering, while not forcing those responsible into a spiral of shame. Obama was nuanced in his presentation, yet simple and accessible, giving me a road map for how I could navigate that space between the moral imperative to do right by everyone and the shame that often stood in our way (Coble, Cobb, Deal & Tuitt, 2013). I saw in him a twenty-first century exemplar for Black leadership that did not need to diminish his racial identity because he transcended race.

While the emerging leader in me had quickly become a fan of Obama's, so too had my father-in-law. This became evident shortly after they met at a Denver bookstore during the promotional tour for Obama's best-selling book, "The Audacity of Hope." I remember asking my father-in-law what he thought of Obama after meeting him in person and he beamed in a way that I had never seen before. He was particularly impressed by Obama's authenticity and humility and was overjoyed when Obama greeted him with an "alright now," signaling to Buckner that he knew that he was in the presence of an elder. He saw Obama as the "real deal" and was willing to believe that he could accomplish what no other Black American could, thereby giving me an opportunity to use his example to prove my father-in-law wrong about Black leadership.

While I was admittedly a fan of Obama's, I tempered my hopes for what his 2008 campaign for the Presidency would accomplish. Although I knew he was incredibly talented and could communicate like no other, like most Black Americans I believed that a Black person would not occupy the Oval Office in my lifetime. While I knew it was inevitable that, eventually, someone other than a White male would occupy the office, I did not feel that this was the time. To me, our nation's proximity to Jim Crow and its emotional legacy was too much to overcome. I was content simply to say I lived at a time when a Black person was the Presidential nominee for a major political party. Having the opportunity to see his speech in person would make it that much sweeter.

So, on August 25, 2008 I stood outside Mile High Stadium in Denver, Colorado alongside my wife, my in-laws, and a few friends to hear Barack Obama deliver his acceptance speech at the Democratic

National Convention. I knew I would be witnessing a great moment in American history, but assumed it was only that: the high point and ultimate end of the Obama campaign. After paying close attention to the long, hard process that he endured to earn the Democratic nomination, I knew that his election was highly unlikely. I figured I would enjoy myself, take a few pictures, and maybe see a few celebrities, then enjoy telling my children about how I'd witnessed that special moment in history. However, as I walked through security and made my way to my seat, my skepticism slowly began to shift. As I looked around the stadium and observed the over 85,000 people in attendance, I started to feel something different. The energy in the building was electric and everyone's joy was unrestrained. It was a scene like nothing I had ever witnessed. All the hate in the world ceased to exist for those few hours. People from all ages, races, and walks of life came from all over the country to witness this "skinny kid" with the funny-sounding name officially accept his nomination for the Presidency of the United States.

While attempting to take it all in, I briefly looked over my right shoulder at my father-in-law. It was clear that he felt as I did. My eyes shifted to the clear blue skies as I thought of my grandparents who had not lived to see this day. Buckner said, "You know what Floyd, he just might pull this off," to which I responded, "You know something, I think you're right." Prior to that moment, I refused to believe that I would see a Black President of the United States in my lifetime; however, the emotions in that stadium on that beautiful August evening suggested that everyone present—and likely a plurality of voters in our country—believed in Barack Obama.

As I watched everyone in attendance proudly waving their American flags and singing along to Stevie Wonder's "Signed, Sealed, Delivered," I knew I was one step closer to accomplishing my goal of proving my father-in-law wrong. I was confident that Barack Obama was going to provide a road map for twenty-first century Black leadership, and with that an opportunity for more Black Americans to be received as positively as he was. I thought that he would change the narrative of negative assumptions about Black America, allowing us to be seen as full members of society, no longer just the country's tolerated step-children. Obama was able to transcend race and make it appear irrelevant, despite the fact that his racial identity was a large part of what made him so appealing.

While I saw Obama's ability to overcome the negativity associated with Blackness as a reflection of his political and leadership talent, others interpreted it as a statement about the racial progress of the United States. Where I viewed him as the embodiment of the twenty-first century Black leader, others saw him as the postracial politician (Bacon Jr. 2007; Williams, 2007). To them, the ascendance of Obama meant that our country had moved beyond race.

Obama vehemently decried the notion of postracialism even before it came to prominence, as expressed in his 2006 book, *The Audacity of Hope*:

> Still when I hear commentators interpreting my speech to mean that we have arrived at a "postracial politics" or that we already live in a color-blind society, I have to offer a word of caution. To say that we are one people is not to suggest that race no longer matters—the fight for equality has been won, or that the problems that minorities face in this country today are largely self-inflicted. On almost every single socioeconomic indicator, from infant mortality to life expectancy to employment to home ownership, Black and Latino Americans in particular continue to lag behind their white counterparts…To suggest that our racial attitudes play no part in these disparities is to turn a blind eye to both our history and our experience—and to relieve ourselves of the responsibility to make things right. (pp. 232–233)

Nonetheless, although Obama quickly made his thoughts about post-racialism known, the momentum behind his symbolism became too much: Postracialism was here to stay. In truth, the emotion surrounding the Obama candidacy in general and the concept of postracialism in particular represented psychological projection (Parker, 2016). People assigned to Obama the hopes and desires that they had for themselves. For many who had been historically disenfranchised, that projection was about the possibility and hope of having our "Americanness" legitimized. Through his ascendancy to the highest office in the land, we could finally be viewed as capable and, most importantly, worthy of everything that America had to offer.

To those who harbored racial bias, post-racialism served as the ultimate redemption of America's meritocratic promise. Obama's success made it possible for some to assume that, in the context of specific opportunities, America is, in fact, colorblind. The fact that we had a Black candidate for President meant that we no longer needed to measure our country "...by sober assessments of how far we have come, but by congratulatory declarations that we have arrived" (Crenshaw, 2011, p. 1314). Moreover, post-racialism as a concept provided these individuals with a moral license (Effron, Cameron, & Monin, 2009; Monin & Miller, 2001) to behave in ways that would have historically not been acceptable because now "we have a Black president." As a result, they could let their prejudicial fears subside and stand proudly on the claim that America is in fact a colorblind meritocracy making it socially permissible to disregard the historical legacy of the state-imposed vulnerability of Black Americans.

This sentiment was captured perfectly on election night in this exchange between TV journalist Anderson Cooper and former Secretary of Education Bill Bennett:

Anderson Cooper: I mean, if he does become President, and it still is an if, does anyone know what this means in terms of change of race relations in the United States, or perception of?

Bill Bennett: Well, I'll tell you one thing it means, as a former Secretary of Education, **you don't take any excuses anymore from anybody who says, "The deck is stacked, I can't do anything, there's so much in-built this and that."** There are always problems in a big society. But we have just—if this turns out to be the case, President Obama—we have just achieved an incredible milestone.

Whether or not one supported Obama, something positive could be taken from his candidacy: Black parents could look their children in the eye and tell them that they could have any career they desired (and mean it) while White Americans exhausted from the shame associated with the legacy of American racism could stand tall and argue confidently that racism was truly a thing of the past. Obama's racial transcendence cut like a double edge sword allowing opponents alike could lay claim to some benefit of his election.

As naïve as it appears now, I was certainly among the many who projected personal hopes onto Obama. While I certainly did not subscribe to the post-racial notion that a Black President led to a racially egalitarian America (Coble, Cobb, Deal, & Tuitt, 2013), I did believe that it signified that Americans in general could truly embrace without reservation the idea of a Black chief executive. While watching his campaign for the nomination, his acceptance speech at Mile High Stadium, and his election night speech in Grant Park, I believed that his presence was a symbol of progress and an opportunity for more Black Americans to live beyond the veil of race (Dubois, 1903/1994) in ways that we never had. I believed that his residence at 1600 Pennsylvania Avenue would, on some level, make things easier for me and other Black leaders in our careers—and give me a clear opportunity to prove my father-in-law wrong.

However, just a short time after Obama was sworn in to the highest office in the land, it became clear that my assumption was misguided. I believed that the presence of a Black President would inject me, as well as my colleagues, with a psychic armor that would make us more immune to racial negativity; instead, I found very quickly that Obama's Presidency would at times make some feel more comfortable to project their negative assumptions about the President upon us. While this reality was impossible for me to conceive during the campaign and inauguration, with all the positive emotions they generated, several subtle incidents in the early months of the Obama Presidency made this apparent. Nothing spoke more clearly to this than the President's first back-to-school speech.

Back to School

On September 8, 2009, President Barack Obama was scheduled to give his first annual back-to-school speech to America's school children. A nonpolitical speech, the premise was simple: encourage students to get off to a good start in the school year, take personal responsibility for their actions, and listen to their parents. Its theme was universal in its application, void of controversy, and utterly benign. The speech was written and delivered to unify our nation's children under one simple cause: to learn for the sake of their country. This was a message that, at first glance, would be hard to dispute and one that any parent would want their child to hear. After all, an educated populace produces economic and social benefits. This should not have been a speech that produced much controversy because it was a concept that Republicans and Democrats alike could get behind.

However, in the days leading up to the speech, the event quickly turned into a national political firestorm. With the health care debate brewing, increasing concerns about the state of the economy and emotions still high from the President's public criticism of the officer who arrested Black Harvard professor Dr. Henry Louis Gates, Jr. in his own home, more Americans were growing comfortable with criticizing our nation's first Black President. Although the fact that the text of the speech was to be made public ahead of time, political opponents and many parents nonetheless slammed the effort as a Hitleresque effort to "indoctrinate" students (Flores & Sims, 2016; MacAskill, 2009; Silverlieb, 2009). They believed that, despite what was written in the simple, benign text, the President was going to deliver messages to their children from which they could never recover.

The truth of what the speech was intended to be simply did not matter. The only thing that did matter was how Barack Obama made a certain group of individuals feel. Logic took a back seat to emotion and no amount of evidence provided was going to change the minds of these individuals leading to parents from across the nation to demand that there be an option for their children to be excused from the President's speech (Flores & Sims, 2016). As a result, educators in school districts across the nation were required to come up with an unprecedented plan to address this concern and my district was no exception.

Fortunately, I worked for a school district that was unafraid to humbly engage in courageous conversations (Singleton & Linton, 2005) about race. While we were by no means perfect, we prided ourselves on bringing to light how our country's racial habits (Glaude, 2016) routinely disenfranchised our minoritized students. Therefore, for many of the leaders in my school district, the racial subtext that surrounded the conversation of the Presidents back to school speech was obvious. Never before had a large group of parents asked to excuse their children from a speech given by the President of the United States, yet under Barack Obama, this appeared to be an entitlement. Where in the past, it was considered our duty to teach children to honor and revere the office of President, now that our President was Black; this rule seemed to no longer apply. It appeared that, whereas in the past, fears of appearing prejudiced might have prevented parents from speaking out on this issue, the moral credentials that post-racialism provided left many feeling immune from those fears. The fact that their stated concerns were unfounded simply did not matter, requiring that we find a way to accommodate this request, independent of how nonsensical it may have seemed.

To address the obvious racial implications of permitting students to "opt out" of a speech by our nation's first Black President, my superintendent convened an emergency meeting of a number of district leaders who known to be the most well versed on issues of race, to think through a potential solution to this problem. Like most other members of this group, I thought the controversy regarding student participation in the speech was utterly absurd and influenced overwhelmingly by race. Nonetheless, in spite of these objections, we all knew that we needed to be responsive to the parents who objected to their children's participation because we had a duty to serve the public requiring us to identify a reasonable solution to meet their demands.

So, amidst our frustration, we worked hard to come up with a system-wide plan to permit students to "opt out" of the President's speech and assuage their parents' concerns about indoctrination. To accommodate this request, principals were required to create a location in their school where students could avoid seeing the speech while it occurred. Once the speech concluded, students would return to class and continue with the daily lesson without the risk of harm to their academic standing. While we were all a bit annoyed by the fact that our world had come to this, we nonetheless felt confident in our plan and believed that we would avoid any major concerns that any parents might have had. Once finished, we made an agreement to reconvene at our regularly scheduled meeting a few days after the speech to debrief on our decision and determine how we might need to adjust in the future. While many of us hoped that this event would be nothing more than an isolated experience, the realization also struck that this could be a sign of things to come.

A few days following the speech, we met at our regularly scheduled time to debrief the effectiveness of our plan as the emotional reaction on the day of the speech seemed minimal in comparison to the excitability that led up to it. So once again, we reconvened in the same room to see if perhaps there was something we had missed. As the conversation began, and the people around the table reported out the things they experienced and heard from other principals, it was clear that the hype leading up to the speech was more isolated than it was far reaching. Despite the media attention, the emotional reaction by some parents, and the incredible amount of time dedicated to preventing Presidential indoctrination, in the end only a handful of students, in a small number of schools decided to take the option to not listen to the speech. For the majority of our principals this incident proved to be a nonissue.

As we continued to debrief our response to this national controversy, the scope of our conversation began to naturally narrow to the schools that had the greatest number of complaints leading up to the speech. While each had done an excellent job in accommodating the parental request, it was the principals at these schools who faced greater amounts of distrust. As I sat there, listened to the conversation, and took account of the names, it was not long before it became self-evident what these principals had in common. While I did not realize it in the days leading up to the speech, in the time period after it became clear that, not coincidentally, that the leaders at these schools were all Black.

Upon realizing this, I immediately reflected upon countless conversations with my father-in-law about his racialized experiences as a leader. I started to wonder if this was an example of the type of

experience he faced because just as he had warned, our Black principals were having qualitatively different experiences than their White
counterparts. While all district leaders were given the same instruc-
tions and completed the same task, the Black leaders were met with a
greater level of skepticism and criticism. Where others were given the
benefit of the doubt, it was our Black leaders who had to contend with
assaults on their integrity. Their title did not matter and the truth did
not matter. The only thing that did was the negative perceptions that
outsiders held in the days leading up to the speech. They could not
transcend race.

While I'm sure it was not truly the case, it appeared that this
indignity was ours alone to suffer, as it was becoming obvious that
one's race determined a leader's level of political vulnerability. As
much as I was hurt by what my father-in-law had told me, it was
clear that he was correct: there were just some people who struggled
with the idea of Black leadership. The election of a Black President
did not matter; in fact, Barack Obama's presence served as proof of
that. As I sat in the meeting, trying to make sense of the obvious
subtext of what we had just experienced, I began to wonder if this
what it might mean for my future and if this was what it meant to
lead while Black. Is this what we must face? Are these the battles that
I need to prepare myself to fight? Am I condemned to deal with this
for the rest of my career? *If so, how do I persist in a post-racial world that
equates the election of a Black President with the attainment of racial justice*
(Crenshaw, 2011)?

My Awakening

In the weeks that followed the incidents surrounding the President's
back-to-school speech, I slowly began to gain a deeper appreciation for
what my father-in-law had told me about some individuals' responses
to Black leadership. While I had a living example whose daily tribula-
tions in the White House I could observe on my television, during my
own professional ascendancy I also gained greater perspective of what
it meant to lead while Black.

At that time, I was a first-year student in the Curriculum and Instruction doctoral program at the University of Denver. Inspired by the election of Barack Obama, I enrolled in the program with the explicit intention of finding the cause of the racial achievement gap. Although I may previously have believed that finding this answer was impossible, the election of our nation's first Black President made it now seem plausible.

I began the program with what I would now consider to be a mediocre understanding of issues of educational equity. I was aware of some of the top theorists, and had command of several trendy phrases, such as *culturally responsive education* and *critical race theory* but, like many doctoral students, when it came to the academic suffering of Black children, I thought I knew more than I actually did. Prior to entering the program, I was fascinated by social psychological research and its related impact on student/teacher relationships and student performance, particularly the intersection of Carol Dweck's mindset theory (2006) with Claude Steele's notion of stereotype threat (1997).

Both theories were extensions of the Pygmalion effect in the classroom, which posited that student achievement was directly related to a teacher's perceived belief in a student's potential to learn (Rosenthal & Jacobson, 1968). Consequently, if students believe that their teacher thinks they can achieve, then a self-fulfilling prophecy will ensue and students will achieve. After studying this work, I was convinced that if I could find a way to place students in courses with teachers who made them feel safe, I could begin the process of closing the achievement gap within my school. All I had to do was to help students find the right teacher fit.

I entered my doctoral program with a plan to use this knowledge to create a professional development plan that would help teachers wake up to this issue. I was confident that once more teachers were made aware of concepts such as growth mindset and stereotype threat, they would take appropriate steps to reduce negative effects and let all children know that they believed in their potential. However, that thinking began to change after I completed a course during my first quarter of enrollment.

The course was called "Introduction to Curriculum and Instruction" and, while offered early in my program, I regard it as the most influential course I've ever taken. The class focused on exposing students to a breadth of curricular theorists with whom we might align philosophically as we began to establish our curricular identities. My professor introduced us to the works of Ralph Tyler (2003), Elliot Eisner, (1996), William Ayers (2001), E. D. Hirsch, (2007) Richard Louv (2008), Sonia Nieto (1999), and Nel Noddings (2005); their varied approaches provided us with new perspectives on curriculum and instruction. While I found benefit and meaning in each of the works, it was not until the seventh week of the course, when I read Sonia Nieto's *The Light in Their Eyes*, that I finally found my curricular identity.

The precision of Nieto's words spoke to me in a way that none of the other authors had. Prior to reading her work, I was convinced that educational inequality and equity should be addressed via teaching methods, student/teacher relationships, and educators' beliefs about students' capacity; however, Nieto's words forced me to question my thinking and consider the impact of unequal access in schools in a way that I could not previously comprehend. This became clear to me after reading the introduction to her book, in which she discussed how educators misunderstand the purpose of multicultural and equity-related programs in schools:

> Curiously missing from discussions in most schools that claim to "do" multicultural education are statements having to do with student learning. The situation was brought out dramatically to me one day many years ago when I was talking with a friend about a multicultural education initiative being implemented in a nearby urban school system. The reservations she had about the project were evident in the question she asked about it, a question remarkable in its simplicity: "But are the kids learning?" she wanted to know. Several years later, another friend struck a similar theme as we were discussing the value of multicultural programs. Of the children who took part in such programs, she asked, "but can they do math?"

> My friends' questions disclosed a concern that schools, in their enthusiasm to provide students with positive role models, to boost self-esteem, and diversify the curriculum (all sorely needed, no question about it), were neglecting their fundamental role: to promote student learning...It is my contention

that questions such as, "But can they do math?" are profoundly multicultural questions because they strike at the very heart of access to learning, and this is where educational inequities are most visible." (Nieto, 1999 pp. xvi–xvii)

Upon reading this passage, I felt like I had been kicked in the chest. Never before had I come across someone who spoke so directly to K–12 educators' failed understanding of the "fundamental role" of equity-related programs. What's more, she did so in such a way that I was forced to include myself in that group of educators. While this was by no means the first time that I had come across a criticism of approaches that focused on students' feelings, there was something utterly jarring about the direct but simple way that she asked this question. "But can they do math?" got to the core of what equity-related research was all about and yet, in spite all of my studies, I had failed to ask it. While my work related to student/teacher relationships was of great importance, that strong bond meant nothing if in the end the students could not read, write, or count. That was the question I had neglected to ask for far too long.

Nieto's question forced me to consider the structural impediments to student learning in a way no other scholar had.

Limited educational opportunities commonly result in poor achievement and lack of learning for individual students, but it is important to stress that unequal outcomes generally are based on students' memberships in particular groups that are ranked according to the status of members' race, ethnicity, social class, and gender among other differences. If this were not the case…the consistent and disproportionate educational failure among American Indians, Latinos, African Americans some Asian Americans, females and poor and working-class students of all ethnic backgrounds would not be a recurring phenomenon. (Nieto, 1999 p. 23)

As I read these words, I began to reflect on my father-in-law's argument about the achievement gap and realized once again that he was correct. This argument of unequal access was presenting itself in the way that he had predicted, forcing me to look at the gap in a new light. While my father-in-law talked about unequal access and its effect on the achievement gap as a matter of fact, Nieto bluntly stated that to ignore this effect was to assume that all student learning experiences were equal, and that the cause of disparate learning outcomes was exclusively the responsibility of the students and not the school (Ladson-Billings, 2006). I knew this was simply not the case.

As I started to delve into additional research, I quickly learned that Nieto was not alone in this belief. I soon found similar perspectives from Darling-Hammond (2010), Ladson-Billings (2006), Oakes (2005; 2011), and even ACT (ACT, 2005a; ACT, 2005b; ACT, 2007; Noble & Schnelker, 2007) who all helped me realize that the facts to what led to this gap were not in question. All of these scholars asserted that standardized test scores were related to the learning opportunities to which students were exposed. The lack of student performance on standardized exams was not so much attributable to cultural bias in the exams but a function of access to coursework, placing the solution to the achievement gap well within my control.

Nieto's book and the subsequent research I explored inspired me to interrogate the effect that unequal access had on the achievement gap in my school. Like most who worked in K-12 education, I was aware of the open secret that learning opportunities in many suburban schools are segregated, with low level and remedial courses disproportionately offered to the poor and to students of color. Before reading Nieto's book, however, I had never considered the effect of those courses on student test score outcomes because, ultimately, most of these students managed to graduate from high school and move on with their lives.

As a budding scholar, I made the decision to take the next step to test the hypothesis the effect of unequal access to coursework on student outcomes in my school. To accomplish this, I compiled data from our assessment office to determine whether course difficulty affected outcomes on our school's annual state-mandated standardized test in mathematics. With nascent statistical competence, I explored the data to assess whether enrollment in an above-grade level math course affected the likelihood of getting a passing score on the standardized exam. While I assumed that students in more challenging classes would have higher average mean scores, I still believed that I would see a normal distribution in all course levels when it came to student proficiency on the exam. However, to my absolute shock, this was not the case.

The preliminary analysis revealed that students enrolled in above-grade level courses such as Geometry, Algebra 2, and Statistics had an exponentially higher likelihood of success than those enrolled in the grade level Algebra course or below grade level courses like Pre-Algebra. Independent of grade earned in the course, the likelihood of a student in an above-grade level course receiving a standardized test score of at least "proficient" on our statewide exams was 90%, whereas those students in courses identified as offering grade level-or-below content had passing rates of 19% and 3%, percent, respectively. What's more, minoritized students were disproportionately enrolled in courses that were less predictive of success, making the achievement gap a predictable phenomenon. The data revealed just what Nieto and my father-in-law had identified: *access mattered profoundly.*

If a teacher had a strong relationship with her students and did not teach at a high enough level, then student performance would not be reflected in standardized test scores. This is not to suggest that relationships do not matter, but that they only do when students enroll in courses predictive of success. This is true because many standardized exams are designed to measure content knowledge and not intellectual ability (Cobb & Russell, 2015). It became clear to me that if my school changed the students' coursework experience, we might stand a better chance of closing the racial performance gap. Without this critical step, the gap would always exist. Therefore, if improved access to coursework and learning experiences predict success, then we could not only close the gap in average performance between racial groups but also increase student achievement across the board for all students. To me this appeared to be a win for everyone involved.

At first glance this appeared to be the perfect "targeted universal" (Powell, 2009) strategy to address the achievement gap. By focusing on increased access to quality learning experiences for all students, instead of narrowly tailored programs that focused on Black students, I felt that I could avoid the constant arguments I faced about privileging the needs of one group of students at the expense of the other. This approach would afford access to quality coursework to *all* students, with an increased magnitude of impact for the historically marginalized. This might shift the focus to the outcome of treatment instead of a stated rhetorical intention to help students of color. Like Obama, I felt like this was the perfect way for a Black leader to address inequality, because it created a frame that was very difficult to debate. As Obama noted:

> The point is that we are able then to make strides on issues that can close the achievement gap, or close the gap on insurance, without calling them targeted programs...they are programs that help people who need help the most. And we do that because it's good for those individuals [and]...it's good for everybody...What I say is, I'm going to create universal programs that make sure everybody's got a shot, but because it provides a ladder of opportunity for everybody it's the people who have got the least opportunity who are going to benefit most from it. And that is consistent not only with concerns about the historically left out; but it's also consistent with what I think a broad base of Americans view as fair and just. That's their definition of equal opportunity... (Dyson, 2016, pp. 160–161)

Because it was the end of November, and the deadline for course selection for the following school year was quickly approaching, I knew that I needed to share my ideas in time to implement the needed changes. While the timeline was tight, I was certain that, once I'd explained the effects of unequal access on student test scores, everyone would have the same epiphany that I had. We would spring into action, taking concrete steps toward addressing this national problem. However, to my dismay, when I shared these findings it became clear that improving equitable access to learning experiences would be more challenging than I could ever imagine.

While many of my colleagues recognized that our practices had contributed to the achievement gap, I was astonished to find that some of them were so dismissive of facts. Where I saw it as absolutely humiliating and a form of educational malpractice to enroll a student in a course that would virtually ensure a failing score on the statewide-standardized test, others suggested that the findings revealed nothing more than the natural intelligence of the students enrolled in the grade level and lower end courses. These colleagues viewed the enrollment of students in courses destined for failure on the annual state exam as "in their best interest," believing that the coursework to which they were being exposed was adequate; this, despite our knowledge that course placement decisions were informed by a teacher's perception as much as by the student's academic performance. They argued that students who were not in advanced courses were not ready for the more challenging workload and should instead be taught study skills; of course, these study skills would be of little use if the students had not been taught enough content. What's more, some argued that placing students in courses that were too rigorous would cheapen the experience for those who had "earned" the right to be enrolled, forcing teachers to teach at a lower level with potential negative test score outcomes for the advanced students.

Before long, the thrill, excitement, and hope that I initially felt turned to frustration as it became increasingly clear that, despite the results of my data analysis, unequal access for our students would not be addressed in the coming year. The educational negligence that I had discovered was slated to continue, leaving me to watch students who looked like me fail our state exam, even though I had evidence that could help them.

What frustrated me most was that I had mountains of evidence and detailed analysis to support my claim of inequality, while numerous colleagues felt entitled to dismiss my findings without offering a single piece of contradictory data. For them, my facts did not matter; the only thing that did was how this evidence made them feel.

Although I had done my research and presented a sound and rational argument that a number of my colleagues supported, the political will just did not exist to make the changes necessary to ensure that all students were given an opportunity to succeed on these exams. Instead of viewing student achievement as an opportunity that could be had by all, some could only see it as a zero-sum enterprise, with the message of equal opportunity being clouded by a messenger who might have a hidden agenda.

In a way, this resistance to addressing equitable course access paralleled the President's troubled attempts to provide healthcare to all Americans. Like Obama, I was seeking a targeted universal approach (Dyson, 2016) aimed at increasing access and opportunity, with an emphasis on those who had historically been left behind, and yet I was experiencing resistance from those looking to protect the individuals who already had these things. Like Obama, I viewed an approach that focused on equal access as one that seemed "fair and just," and yet it was clear that there were some people who did not share our definition.

Quite naturally, as I met this wall of resistance, I was forced once again to confront the reality of my father-in-law's statements about the challenges of Black leadership. Like him, I occupied a leadership role in a school, with the perceived authority to influence my school's academic direction—and yet I was not being heard. Like him I had an incredible depth of knowledge related to the issue that I wanted to address, but still felt utterly helpless in my efforts to eradicate the academic suffering of students who looked like me.

While it was certainly frustrating to have my facts dismissed, it was totally devastating to see my reflection in the eyes of those colleagues who believed in me. It was obvious that they believed my ideas were solid, my intentions pure, and my rationale sound; they also recognized that I was being professionally invalidated in a way that was at least tangentially related to my racial identity. Without saying a word, these colleagues gazed at me with pity and irritation as they bore witness to my professional humiliation.

This experience left me feeling professionally discouraged and searching for answers. Although I was self-assured in my findings and confident in my work, I still felt despair due to my constant struggle to close my school's achievement gap. I worked in an organization with the stated mission and goals of improving academic outcomes for all students, and yet trying to do just that seemed like a constant battle. While practically everyone would publicly claim that they believed that all students deserved a quality learning experience, few were willing to make the structural decisions that would actually support this outcome. They wanted things to improve, yet they wanted nothing to change, the implication being that it was the students who simply were not doing their part.

As the Obama era progressed and I moved into school leadership, the power of my father-in-law's statement began to have greater meaning; it was clear to me that, in this instance, he had proven himself right. As the impact of not being heard increased, so too did my double consciousness (Dubois, 1903/1994). Instead of viewing myself as I wanted to be seen, I could only see myself "through the eyes of others" (Dubois, 1903/1994)—and these eyes looked at me and my efforts to achieve racial equality with disdain and contempt. Prior to the Obama election, my voice on matters of inequality was largely unchallenged; now I was experiencing a professional silencing that caused me self-conscious pain. Caught in an impossible situation, I saw myself as someone striving to end the suffering of children who looked like me, while being discouraged from doing so. I felt trapped and verbally constrained, leaving me experiencing a professional "two-ness" (Dubois, 1903/1994) in a way that was totally new.

Although as a Black man I knew all too well the experience of being "two souls, two thoughts, two reconciled strivings; two warring ideals in one dark body" (Dubois, 1903), professionally, I felt that I was now being asked to play a new role. While I, like other Black Americans, had routinely been taught that I had to be twice as good to get half as far as White Americans in this world, the strategic moral credentials now being offered in this post-racial era left me wondering if I was now also being asked to be "half as Black" (Coates, 2012). Where I wanted the freedom to be the person I knew I could be and take radical steps to address academic inequality with the "fierce urgency of now" (King, 1967), it was clear that doing so in the context of the stereotypical assumptions about my racial identity could lead many to perceive me as being *too Black*. Instead of the critical leader I knew myself to be, I felt like I was being coerced to perform a more racially palatable "working identity" (Carbado & Gulati, 2015), despite the fact that doing so meant that the children I wanted to support would continue to fall short of their learning potential.

This tension left me worn down, fatigued, and strained in a way that was all too familiar. While I was still being treated in my personal life with the skepticism, fear, and mistreatment that are associated with being a Black man in America, in my professional life I was encouraged to behave as if that experience was utterly unfamiliar. In a sense, I felt the post-racial moral license gave some individuals permission to look upon me as if I were no longer Black, although most knew nothing of how it felt to "be a problem" (Dubois, 1903) in a dark body in the country of your birth.

References

ACT (2005a). *What kind of test preparation is best?* Iowa City, IA: ACT Policy Report.

ACT (2005b). *Courses count: Preparing students for postsecondary success.* Iowa City, IA: ACT Policy Report.

ACT (2007). *Technical manual.* IA: ACT Policy Report.

Bacon, P., Jr. (2007, January). Can Obama count on the Black vote? *Time Magazine.* Retrieved from http://content.time.com/time/nation/article/0,8599,1581666,00.html

Carbado, D. W., & Gulati, M. (2013). *Acting white?: Rethinking race in post-racial America.* London: Oxford University Press.

Coates, T. N. (2012). Fear of a Black president. *The Atlantic.* Retrieved from http://www.theatlantic.com/magazine/archive/2012/09/fear-of-a-black-president/309064/

Coble, B., Cobb, F., Deal, K., & Tuitt, F. (2013). Navigating the space between Obama and the postracial myth. In D. J. C. Andrews & F. Tuitt (Eds.), *Contesting the myth of a "post-racial era": The continued significance of race in US education* (pp. 25–41). New York, NY: Peter Lang.

Crenshaw, K. W. (2010). Twenty years of critical race theory: Looking back to move forward. *Connecticut Law Review, 43,* 1253.

Darling-Hammond, L. (2010). *The flat world and education: How America's commitment to equity will determine our future.* New York, NY: Teachers College Press.

DuBois, W. E. B. (1994). *The souls of Black folk.* New York, NY: Dover Publications. (Original Work published 1903.)

Effron, D. A., Cameron, J. S., & Monin, B. (2009). Endorsing Obama licenses favoring whites. *Journal of Experimental Social Psychology, 45*(3), 590–593.

Flores, L. A., & Sims, C. D. L. (2016). The aero-sum game of race and the familiar strangeness of President Obama. *Southern Communication Journal, 81*(4), 206–222.

Glaude, E. S., Jr. (2016). *Democracy in black: How race still enslaves the American soul.* New York, NY: Crown.

Hanna, D. P. (1988). *Designing organizations for high performance*. New York, New York: Addison-Wesley Publishing Company.

MacAskill, E, (2009, September 8). Schools boycott Obama speech as critics abruptly change tone *The Guardian*. Retrieved from https://www.theguardian.com/world/2009/sep/08/obama-school-speech-boycott-protest

Monin, B., & Miller, D. T. (2001). Moral credentials and the expression of prejudice. *Journal of Personality and Social Psychology, 81*, 33–43.

Oakes, J. (2005). Keeping track: How schools structure inequality, 2nd edition. Yale University Press.

Oakes, J. (2011). The distribution of knowledge. In R. Arum, I. Beattie, & K. Ford, (Eds.), *The structure of schooling: readings in the sociology of education* (pp. 199–207). Pine Forge Press.

Obama, B. (2004). Keynote address: Democratic national convention. Retrieved from http://www.washingtonpost.com/wp-dyn/articles/A19751-2004Jul27.html

Obama, B. (2007). *The audacity of hope: Thoughts on reclaiming the American dream*. New York, NY: Three Rivers Press.

Silverleib, A. (2009, September 5). Many conservatives enrages over Obama school speech. CNN. Retrieved from http://www.cnn.com/2009/POLITICS/09/04/obama.schools/

Singleton, G. E. (2014). *Courageous conversations about race: A field guide for achieving equity in schools*. Thousands Oakes, CA: Corwin Press.

Williams, J. (2001, November 30). Obama's color line. *The New York Times*. Retrieved from http://www.nytimes.com/2007/11/30/opinion/30williams.html?_r=1

Chapter 2

Between Carlton Banks and *Django Unchained*: Racism as Humiliation

I learned that to humiliate another person is to make him suffer an unnecessarily cruel fate.

—*Nelson Mandela, 1976*

On Becoming Carlton

The perceived requirement to mask my racial identity while being told in subtle ways that I was *too Black* touched a nerve with me because it contrasted with the experiences of my youth. As I noted in the introduction, much of my life has been informed by the stress and trauma of being the only Black person in many environments and consequently, I was frequently told that I was *not Black enough*.

Having grown up as one of the few Black children in my suburban San Diego community, the pain of having my racial authenticity challenged was an all-too-common experience. Therefore, to experience this at work felt aggravatingly familiar but simultaneously confounding because it placed me in a racial double-bind that was entirely foreign. I've come to know the fatigue, anxiety, and exhaustion of racial isolation: the pain of being viewed as an object instead of a human, the sting felt after hearing comments about my inauthentically Black accent, and the agony of carrying the representational weight of all things Black in an effort to defy stereotypes. I know quite well what it feels like to be that person. However, to be indirectly told that my actions were too Black was new to me, and was likely a residual effect of my undergraduate experiences.

While I explored undergraduate options during high school, I sought out a Historically Black College and University (HBCU). I understood that doing so meant moving away from my native state of California, but I was unconcerned as I wanted to experience what it was like to be in the racial majority. I knew attending an HBCU would give me a chance to blend in instead of standing out; a chance to just be me and not a symbol of a race that is as culturally diverse as it is complex; a chance to take a momentary break from the daily stress of being the only or the Other; and an opportunity to fit in as others take for granted. Consequently, I applied to Morehouse College, Southern University, North Carolina A&T State University, Grambling State University, and Howard University. I considered the predominantly White institutions to which I applied as "safety schools." As a first-generation college student, I was obviously nervous and somewhat bewildered by the complexity of the collegiate application process; nonetheless, I was admitted to all but one of the institutions to which I applied. I was now in the driver's seat. My hard work in high school had paid off and, because of it, I was given the opportunity to choose the institution of my liking. My choice was clear: I would be going to the Mecca, Howard University.

Upon letting my friends and family know about my decision to attend Howard, those familiar with the school frequently commented that I was in for a "culture shock." After all, I was a kid from San Diego, moving to pregentrified northwest Washington, DC. I was literally moving from the safe and spacious enclaves of my suburban neighborhood, where it seemed that everyone knew my name, to a crowded inner city with more Black Americans living within a city block than I might see at home in an entire year.

To be honest, I had no idea what culture shock meant, so when I heard the phrase I would nod, smile, and express my excitement while pretending I understood. I assumed that things would not be much different than where I grew up in California except for the fact that everyone would be Black. The myriad of ways of how the culture of an HBCU campus in the heart of Washington, D.C., would be any different from my suburban Southern California neighborhood did not occur to me. I was focused on living in an environment that was predominantly Black not having a full understanding of what that meant. All I was concerned with was having a chance for the first time in my life to be my authentic self, living free of the racial vulnerability that so routinely dominated my life, and to become a part of that unapologetic Blackness on parade that I knew as Howard University (Coates, 2016).

However, when I arrived on the Howard University campus I slowly began to discover exactly what everyone meant by culture shock. While practically every student on campus was Black, that simple racial designation in no way reflected the degree of cultural diversity within my race. Students descended on that campus from every part of the country and multiple corners of the world, forcing me to reassess my understanding of what it meant to be Black.

Depending upon whether one was from New York, Atlanta, Miami, Virginia, Chicago, or the Caribbean, it was easy to see how we were all different. Everyone had their own style of dress, spoke with different accents, and used different slang, yet we were all Black. My first week on that campus was unlike anything that I had ever experienced in my life, as for the first time I was given an opportunity to understand the full dimensions of my racial identity while being totally unafraid to do so.

Upon settling in to my new home, it became clear that I was not alone in my fascination with the regional differences in Blackness; my new classmates were equally as enamored with the cultural differences that existed between us. While I was particularly infatuated with my friends from the south and the east coast, one of the questions I was repeatedly asked was, "Why do you talk so proper?" Utterly unaware of my quintessentially suburban Southern California accent, I usually responded, "I don't know, this is just how I talk." While I knew my accent was dissimilar to that of my new friends from Virginia, Maryland, Florida, and Illinois, my dialect seemed normal to me. My friends' initial question would typically be followed up with the statement, "You sound like a White person when you talk." I was always perplexed when I heard this, because I did not sound like many of the White kids I knew, many of whom spoke in the surfer dialect unique to Southern California's beach communities. I did not frequently use words like "dude," "awesome," "rad," or "bro." My slang was the urban slang of the day, although to them it may not have sounded authentic. It was clear that I sounded different, and I was okay with that.

The issue of my accent remained a puzzle until I spent a weekend in Virginia with my roommate's family. His Southern accent was in clear contrast to mine, causing the conversation about my accent to resurface with his family when his mother asked, "You know who you remind me of?" After a quizzical glance, I said "I don't know, who?", to which she responded, "You remind me of Carlton," the character from the 90's sitcom, *The Fresh Prince of Bel Air.*

While my friends laughed at the comparison, I cringed. I detested Carlton and wanted nothing to do with the character or what he represented. I could accept that I sounded different; I could even accept the fact that the character and I had the same haircut and were both from California, but I did not want to be associated with or have anything to do with the Carlton. However, from the perspective of my East Coast friends, the similarities were obvious: Like Carton, I was not very tall, I spoke with a West Coast accent, grew up in the suburbs, and had a muscular build. It was easy to see—despite my contempt for him—how the connection could be made.

The physical and regional parallels were obvious; nonetheless, I was still mortified by the connection. My decision to attend Howard University was based on a desire to align with my racial identity, so

I certainly did not want to have my identity aligned with a character who disassociated himself from Blackness. Carlton was the opposite of who I wanted to be.

As portrayed by Alfonso Ribeiro, Carlton was a living reflection of the world's perception of him. Amplified by his naiveté, Carlton was the constant target of humiliation by the other characters, who viewed him as a joke and an easy mark. He was so beautifully unwitting that viewers almost believed that he deserved to be pitied. Famed for his cardigan sweaters, bow ties, and awkward dancing, Carlton was never "Black enough." In fact, he was completely oblivious of racial context. He was certain that his wealth and connections made him impervious to racial vulnerability allowing him to transcend race; although, the show's other characters believed that it was their job to remind him of that racial reality. While aggravating, these traits also made Carlton memorable and endearing, and his story line played itself out repeatedly during the show's successful run. The sixth episode of the first season provided perhaps the best example of Carlton's naiveté.

Mistaken Identity

In the episode titled "Mistaken Identity," Carlton's uncle Phil's law firm partner, Henry Furth, asked him to drive his Mercedes-Benz from Los Angeles to Palm Springs. Mr. Furth and his wife would travel to Palm Springs via helicopter, but needed a car to drive once they arrived. Ever the opportunist, Carlton jumped at this offer, which he believed might result in a future internship opportunity for him.

Carlton set out for Palm Springs in the Mercedes, entertaining himself by singing the Glenn Miller Orchestra's "I Got a Gal in Kalamazoo." En route, he is surprised to discover his cousin Will hiding in the back seat. Mortified by Will's presence, Carlton demands that his cousin behave properly on the trip so as not to undermine Carlton's opportunity to impress Mr. Furth. Will reluctantly agrees, but pesters Carlton like an irritating little brother for the rest of the ride.

After a short stop at a gas station, Carlton makes a wrong turn off the freeway and gets lost. When he reduces his speed to read an approaching street sign, his "suspiciously" slow driving alerts a nearby police officer, who pulls the Mercedes over.

At first, Carlton is thrilled to see the police officer, whom he believes will assist them in returning to the freeway. He assumed that their slow speed was simply an indicator to the officer that they needed assistance. The streetwise Will, however, is petrified, realizing that two young Black men driving a Mercedes will appear suspicious to the officer. The car is not registered to either of them, so they might easily be accused of "fitting the description." Will, who grew up in Philadelphia, has been through this before and knows that one false move might lead to their arrest. Therefore, he responds in a cautious, nonthreatening way to the officer, while Carlton, oblivious to the racial dynamic, proceeds as if it's obvious that they are simply doing a favor for someone. The men end up being arrested on suspicion of stealing the car.

Scared and humiliated, Will uses his wits to alert Carlton's parents to their arrest. Despite the terror of being locked in a cell with other criminals, Carlton remains confident that their arrest was simply a case of mistaken identity and could have happened to anyone. Unconvinced, Carlton's parents were enraged, certain that the arrest was an obvious case of racial profiling. They were sure that, had it not been for the fact that they were Black, the two would have been left alone. Carlton's parents were humiliated that they had to save their innocent child from the crime of driving while Black.

What was obvious to everyone else was incomprehensible to Carlton, who stood firm in his belief that "the police were just trying to do their job" (Borowitz & Borowitz, 1990). He believed that, aside from the mild inconvenience of being arrested and subsequently saved by his legally astute parents, the world is fair and "the system worked" (Borowitz, & Borowitz, 1990) once the officers were provided with the right facts. To Carlton, it was clear that they were pulled over for driving too slow and that he could avoid future encounters with the police by simply "bringing a map" (Borowitz & Borowitz, 1990) because truth always prevailed. He was convinced that the indignities they had experienced were purely coincidental and not a function of race, despite his family's contrary beliefs. This final exchange of the episode is illustrative:

Carlton: Dad, if you were a policeman, and you saw someone driving a car at two miles an hour, wouldn't you stop it?

Philip: I asked myself that question the first time I was stopped. Good night, son. (*He goes upstairs.*)

Carlton: I would stop it. (Borowitz, & Borowitz, 1990)

While the Carlton moniker did not stick with me in college beyond that conversation with my friend's mom, I have never been far from anger when anyone (aside from my friend's mom) attempted to associate me with him because questioning my racial authenticity is an insult. I have always been intent on preserving my dignity instead of being seen as a source of entertainment to those around me. I am not oblivious to my racial context and I am unwilling to tolerate humiliation. Moreover, I know how it feels to be Black, understand deeply the assumptions, trauma and vulnerability that come along with this identity in America, and most importantly, I am a real human being and not a TV character. Given this, when someone suggests that I need to be inauthentically Black, I know they are trying to humiliate me, leaving me feeling racially offended in an all-too-familiar way.

Racism as Humiliation

The verb "humiliate" is defined as "to reduce to a lower position in one's own eyes or others' eyes" (humiliate, 2016) which, according to William Ian Miller (1993), transitioned to its current meaning around the year 1757. Regarded as "a profound, and some-times unspeakable, relational violation," humiliation "draws into doubt one's worth as a human being" (Hartling, Lindner, Spalthoff, & Britton, 2013, p. 60), creating a psychological impact that forces people to question their inherent worth. Born out of contempt, humiliation divides "social groups into two distinct classes: the superior and the inferior" (Fisk, 2001, p. 81).

According to Klein (1991), humiliation requires the participation of three roles: the perpetrator, the vulnerable target, and the witness. When this trifecta is in place and the vulnerable target's dignity is wounded, humiliation results. The emotions associated with humiliation are intense and cognitively debilitating (Fernández, Saguy, & Halperin, 2015; Otten & Jonas, 2015) because of the witness. Consequently, targets of humiliation have been known to descend into depression, have severe anxiety disorders, and even commit suicide (Torres & Bergner, 2010). Humiliation is quite possibly the perfect tool of psychological control, making it an incredibly useful arrow in the quiver of those who seek to oppress.

While humiliation is similar to guilt and shame in that it results in a devalued sense of identity of the target, it is a distinct emotion in its own right. Where guilt and shame are considered intrapersonal emotions that manifest autonomously, humiliation is regarded as interpersonal (Fisk, 2001) and a result of the behavior of another person. Moreover, humiliation requires the perception of unjust treatment, whereas guilt and shame result in an internalized justification for the emotion (Fernández, Saguy, & Halperin, 2015). For a target to be humiliated, there must be a profound belief that the negative treatment received from the perpetrator is unfairly applied, whereas those who feel guilt and shame believe they deserve to feel as they do. Sufferers of humiliation frequently state, "I've done nothing to deserve this," while victims of guilt and shame on the other hand respectively attest "I feel bad for what I've done" or "I am a bad human being" (Brown, 2012). Interestingly, being the repeated target of humiliation can lead to feelings of shame, which in turn cause the psychological trauma. This subtle but critical distinction is what gives humiliation its overwhelming power.

Humiliation is among the most deeply felt emotions (Otten & Jonas, 2014). It hurts, and the powerlessness it produces leads to rage (Linder, 2006). Linder (2006) has referred to humiliation as the "nuclear bomb of emotions" (p. xiii), causing great anger in its sufferers. Moreover, the observation of that rage and incapacity gives satisfaction and gratification to the perpetrator (Fisk, 2013; Sullivan, 2006; Takahasi et al., 2009).

Humiliation cannot occur without injustice and no institution in American history was more unjust or created a greater sense of racial inferiority than that of chattel slavery. Since anti-Black racism originated with slavery, it is not surprising that racism and humiliation are the perfect "silent partners" (Griffin, 1991, p. 151). Humiliation is the behavioral manifestation of racism. Racism is paralyzing and the hurtful slurs that often accompany it produce anger and rage. Moreover, slavery is a system of institutional humiliation—filled with laws, practices, behaviors, and discursive actions—that creates the emotional cascade that individual humiliation also produces.

While racism is the ultimate act of injustice, perpetrators have routinely sought justification for their behaviors. Whether supported through concocted interpretations of the Bible (Omi & Winant, 2015), the pseudoscience of eugenics (Valencia, 2010), or statistical racism (Zuberi, 2008), those who choose to deliberately engage in racial discrimination are constantly in search of a rationale for their irrational behavior. To the perpetrators of racism, the world is just and the United States of America is as fair as the principles on which it was founded. Consequently, those who make accusations of racism and discrimination are routinely discounted because their words violate previously held conceptions about our country.

Hanson and Hanson (2006) argued that Americans "crave justice" and believe in the inherent fairness of the United States, leading many to suffer a form of cognitive bias that Lerner (1980) called the Just World Fallacy. Those who subscribe to this fallacy believe on a fundamental level that bad things do not happen to good people. They instead create "an illusion of justice through assumptions, arguments, or stereotypes about the blameworthiness of the victim" (Hanson & Hanson, 2006, p. 417). Therefore, when claims of racial discrimination are made, those who believe in the Just World Fallacy attempt to rationalize their behavior in order to maintain their understanding of the world. Consequently, targets of racism are charged with the psychologically exhausting task of disproving their worthiness as a target (Darley & Latane, 1968; Salmivalli, 2010). However, for witnesses to consider the perspective of the individual or group being humiliated, the targets must prove to the witnesses that they are not truly inferior by appearing "perfect." Absent perfection, targets of racial humiliation are likely to be disregarded (Figure 2.1).

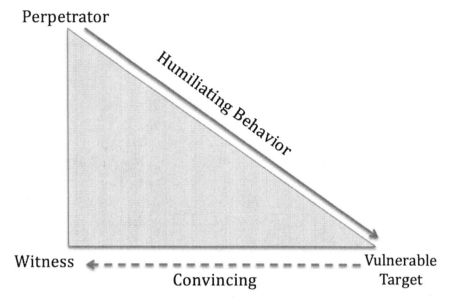

Figure 2.1—Humiliation/Bullying Process.
Source: Adapted from "School-wide intervention in the childhood bullying triangle" by McNamee, A., 2008. Childhood Education 84(6), pp. 371–372.

This unfortunate reality helps explain the need, success, and brilliance of the non-violence strategy deployed during the Civil Rights movement. As leaders, their goal was to achieve civil rights by revealing the humiliating reality of segregation and Jim Crow. The movement's leaders, while fully aware of the social impact of undeniable humiliation and injustice (Cobb, 2012), chose not to fight humiliation with humiliation. Instead, as targets, they sought to outwit the perpetrators by constructing scenarios that made their victimhood unassailable. As Martin Luther King (1964) explained:

> Violence is impractical because it is a descending spiral ending in destruction for all. It is immoral because it seeks to humiliate the opponent rather than win his understanding: It seeks to annihilate rather than convert. Violence is immoral because it thrives on hatred rather than love. It destroys community

and makes brotherhood impossible. It leaves society in monologue rather than dialogue. Violence ends up defeating itself. It creates bitterness in the survivors and brutality in the destroyers…It seeks to secure moral ends through moral means. Nonviolence is a powerful and just weapon. Indeed, it is a weapon unique in history, which cuts without wounding and ennobles the man who wields it.

The movement's leaders relied on passive techniques to create circumstances where the media could illustrate injustice; for example, by providing footage of human beings helplessly sprayed by water hoses or attacked by police dogs while marching for their rights. While passive, the creation of these circumstances was critical because these images' inhumanity made it impossible for witnesses to justify or ignore them. The brilliance of the nonviolent strategy of the Civil Rights movement was that it made the victimization of the Black protestors indisputable and the truth inarguable.

This helps explain why Rosa Parks was deliberately chosen as the antisegregation test case for the National Advancement for the Association of Colored People (NAACP) in 1955. Contrary to popular belief, she was not a singular figure in her act of civil disobedience in refusing to give up her seat to a White patron. Aurelia Browder, Claudette Colvin, Mary Louise Smith, and Susie McDonald (Browder v. Gayle, 1956) all engaged in similar acts prior to Parks, but she was selected as the face of the movement because she was closest to perfect. Parks' personal credentials were impeccable and her pristine background made her incredibly difficult to discredit, lending validity to the broader cause. While Colvin, for instance, had experienced an unwed pregnancy, making her far from perfect, Parks had done nothing to deserve her treatment "except to be born Black" (Parks & Haskins, 1992, p. 125). Therefore, to outsiders, Parks could be viewed as the perfect target who, through public suffering, created a compassionate context for the inhumanity of segregation. In doing so, Civil Rights leaders made injustice obvious and the facts indisputable helping clarify the humanity of Black Americans for the whole world to see.

Unfortunately, the perfect victim rarely exists and the constant vigilance required to predict perpetrators' actions is psychologically taxing, making the dynamic of racism and humiliation so powerful. Moreover, the requirement of perfection allows witnesses to dismiss racism whenever the victim appears flawed and, therefore, "undeserving" of compassion. This impossibly high standard keeps the target on guard against future attempts at denigration, resulting in mental anguish and rage. This mindset permeates all facets of our culture, extending into our social, institutional, and even educational worlds. While not always obvious, this undercurrent is ever present because this mindset is so foundational to our society.

In the educational setting, the dynamic of racism and humiliation is revealed though traditional structures, processes, and discourses (Yosso, 2002). Known as the hidden curriculum, Giroux and Penna (1979) regarded this dynamic as "the unstated norms, values and beliefs that are transmitted to students through the underlying structure of meaning in both the formal content as well as the social relations of school and classroom life" (p. 22). In this hidden curriculum, "values shape and influence practically every aspect of the student's educational experience" (p. 32), teaching students implicit and explicit messages. Griffin (1991) revealed how the humiliating component of the schools' hidden curriculum manifests as individual, institutional, and cultural racism. In the following subsections, I describe each construct in detail, while offering contemporary and personal examples of how each are applied.

Individual Racial Humiliation

Griffin (1991) defined individual racism as the racially based "attitudes, beliefs, and behaviors that occur in interactions between individuals" (p. 150) that are revealed in antipathy and contempt for a racially similar group. It results in the explicit denial of opportunity simply because of race. This definition is the one that likely dominates the American psyche whenever the word "racism" is uttered. It is public and allows the perpetrator to disregard and humiliate their target simply because of race.

Individual racism likely conjures up thoughts of public punishments like whippings, lynchings, and mutilations, or perhaps the burning of crosses and similar activities fixated on producing fear and maintaining physical and psychological control of the intended target. Individual racism seeks to deny human dignity by affecting the psyches of its targets and bystanders whose identities are similarly aligned. It is cold, heartless, and a public display of racial humiliation. History is filled with countless examples of this type of racial denigration deployed on Black Americans, starting with the treatment of enslaved Africans.

Christian and Bennett (1998) suggested that overseers and plantation owners used individual racism and humiliating tactics to achieve the "ideal slave." Overseers were certain (Christian & Bennett, 1998; Zinn, 2016) that if they controlled the minds of enslaved Africans, they could also control their behavior. Confident in their methods, they created a list of techniques to be shared amongst fellow overseers to ensure psychological control over the enslaved (Christian & Bennett, 1998; Zinn, 2016). The list included five simple concepts that, when routinely applied, were likely to cause humiliation and shame. First, the overseers were to ensure that enslaved Africans were to "obey at all times, *in all circumstances* (emphasis mine), cheerfully and with alacrity" to ensure "unconditional submission" (Christian & Bennet, 1998, p. 144). Second, overseers were to create a sense of personal inferiority in the enslaved Africans when compared to any White person, so that they would always "know their place" (Christian & Bennet, 1998). Third, overseers were to instill a sense of fear in the hearts and minds of the enslaved Africans to keep them astonished by their overseers' power. Fourth, the enslaved Africans were required to take an interest in their master's enterprise to ensure financial gain. Fifth and finally, the overseers needed to ensure that their enslaved Africans "remained ignorant of all things that would encourage independence" (p. 144). Thus, they were deprived of education and encouraged to engage in "simple entertainment," which left them completely helpless. The combination of these techniques kept many enslaved Africans metaphorically shackled, even when the braces were not physically applied, leading to the development of a culture of internalized oppression (Woodson, 1933).

These five techniques proved incredibly successful and had latent effects for generations to come; in many cases, the enslaved did not realize that they were treated as chattel. The consequences of such inhumane treatment led to the miseducation (Woodson, 1933) of Black Americans and other races. After decades of unchallenged oppression, Americans of all races have become conditioned (Fanon, 1967) to believe (many times in the subconscious) that Black Americans were worthy of this treatment, leading to belief systems that pervade our country today.

While public deployment of individual racism is no longer socially, politically, or legally acceptable, it has not disappeared. The entitlement to humiliate and the psychic benefits that accompany that action remain; however, the act takes on a much subtler—though no less insidious—form. Today, individual racism is most likely to appear in the form of microaggressions. This term, first coined by Chester Pierce (1970), and most recently attributed to Sue (2010; Sue et al., 2007; Sue, Capodilupo, & Holder, 2008) and Solórzano (Kohli & Solórzano 2012; Ledesma & Solórzano, 2013; Solorzano, Cela, & Yosso, 2000), refers to brief and commonplace daily verbal, behavioral, or environmental indignities, whether intentional or unintentional, that communicate hostile, derogatory, or negative racial slights and insults toward people of color (Sue et al., 2007).

Although less overtly violent in form, perpetrators of racial microaggressions deliver "subtle and stunning insults" (Solorzano et al., 2000) that are not too different from those sent to enslaved Africans. Microaggressions are implied indignities that communicate a sense of superiority that "support racial and cultural hierarchy of minority inferiority on the part of the perpetrator" (Kohli & Solórzano, 2012, p. 441). Racial microaggressions seek to ensure that the targets "know their place." With comments like "You're so articulate for a Black person," "You're pretty for a dark-skinned girl," or "Did you get this job because of Affirmative Action?," racial microaggressions communicate to the intended targets that they have lower social status and are worthy of humiliation.

The power of racial microaggressions lies in their subtlety and repetition. The less obvious nature of these insults, coupled with their frequency, makes the pain and injustice encountered more challenging to explain to witnesses who are not in tune with the experience. This is especially true when compared to overt racial discrimination. The ambiguity of the suffering and indignity allow the experience to be easily denied and attributed to a miscommunication or oversensitivity (Sue, Capodilupo, & Holder, 2008). This denial of reality is suffocating, and the constant cycle of microaggression, indignity, and denial produces emotions identical to those resulting from humiliation. While less obvious than in the past, racial microaggressions are the twenty-first century manifestation of individual racism. In a sense, microaggressions are nothing more than a never-ending series of microhumiliations.

Individual Racial Humiliation in K–12 Schools

In the K–12 context, the linkage between individual racism, microaggressions, and humiliation is unmistakable, particularly in the context of student-teacher interactions (Allen, 2010; Kohli & Solórzano, 2012). With the added component of the power differential between the teacher and the student, microaggressions in the educational context can prove especially devastating. When deployed by teachers toward their students, microaggressions leave the targets feeling even more powerless than in a typical social interaction. In the classroom, the teacher has a disproportionate amount of power and the ability to control the destiny of a student. This unequal relationship makes it difficult for students to offer a challenge against subtle insults.

Therefore, when microaggressions manifest, such as when a Black student enters an Honors class and the teacher's first words are, "Are you sure you belong in this class?," students are forced to negotiate the social cost of enduring such an insult, coupled with the exhausting, complicated task of explaining the injustice to their peer witnesses. Not dissimilar to the tactics deployed to create the "ideal slave," microaggressions pose the question "Do you belong here?" and, if so, "know that you need to behave as I say at all times" and be sure to "stay in your place." Whether the teacher intends to demean the student in this case is immaterial. Black students are more likely to be on guard against attempts at humiliation.

In the K–12 environment, the desire to control student behavior via racial microaggressions occurs most frequently in the context of classroom management. Simply put, when it comes to student discipline, "race is not neutral" (Skiba et al., 2011, p. 85) and in the context of zero-tolerance policies, these microaggressions lead to disparate treatment of Black students (Okonofua & Eberhardt, 2015). Research repeatedly reveals that Black students are more likely to be considered "disruptive" than other students (Wright, 2015). Additionally, Black students are disciplined more frequently and harshly than other racial groups, and for more subjective reasons, such as disrespect, loitering, disruption, and talking loudly (Skiba et al, 2002). Scholars have found that Black students are routinely suspended and expelled at higher rates, even when they make up a representational minority in the school (Skiba et al., 2011; Smith & Harper, 2015). The result of such disproportionality has an academic impact and compounds achievement disparity issues between racial groups (Gregory, Skiba, & Noguera, 2010; Morris & Perry, 2016).

As a school leader who was responsible for discipline for several years, I experienced this reality firsthand. As a disciplinarian, I executed policies that led to the racially disproportionate rates of suspension and expulsion in my schools. While not proud of this, I had to operate within the confines of what many of our zero tolerance policies required. I had to do my job even though that meant that a higher number of students who looked like me would be suspended.

Throughout my tenure in these positions, I frequently encountered Black students who were sent to my office by their teachers for nonspecific infractions including noncompliance, defiance, and disrespect. These infractions were almost always due to an interpersonal issue between the student and the teacher. When I would ask the teacher what led to the class dismissal, I frequently heard explanations such as, "I'm tired of warning him/her" or "You need to talk to him/her about how to behave in school." I then asked the teacher whether a parent had been contacted about the student's numerous warnings. This typically led to a series of stammering statements followed by a very slow "no." In almost every case, I would immediately send the student back to class with a direction to the teacher to not send students to my office without contacting a parent.

However, in rare cases, I would find that I could not send the student immediately back to class. In these instances, the teacher had provoked the student into doing something that was against the rules, such as using foul language. In short, the teacher would set the student up. When the student arrived at my office after this type of interaction, he/she would always be enraged. I made it a point to give him/her an opportunity to settle down and gather his/her thoughts so I could learn what happened. When asked the source of the conflict from his/her perspective, in far too many instances the student simply replied that the teacher "was racist."

Inevitably, I would ask what the teacher specifically did for the student to make such an egregious claim. I was fully aware that calling a teacher "racist" was a harsh accusation that would require a lot of evidence to justify. Paralyzed by my response, most students would helplessly shrug their shoulders and say, "I don't know, I can't explain it, it's not anything specific, I just know." The students were attempting to tell me that their teacher routinely and repeatedly indicated (consciously and/or subconsciously) that, as a Black American, they were worthy of humiliation. Moreover, the students would implicitly state that "I don't have the right words to name my pain (Ledesma & Solórzano, 2013, p. 118), making it impossible for me to prove this claim, but I know what I'm feeling and it hurts."

Institutional Racial Humiliation

Griffin (1991) stated that institutional racism "has become a part of the formal and informal policies and practices of the educational, religious, political, economic, health, recreational and other systems of society" (p. 151). This type of racial discrimination is structural in form and uses the power of institutions to oppress. Operating on the premise that the historical treatment of all persons in this country was just, institutional racism relies upon the theory of meritocracy to enact humiliation. This form of discrimination is postracial and ignores historical context for current outcomes, encouraging perpetrators to ask questions such as, "Why don't you all just pull yourselves up by your bootstraps?"

Institutional racism has deep roots in the United States. It is present in many contexts, but is most prominently seen through the application of Jim Crow laws. In the post-reconstruction United States, Black Americans, in spite of their citizenship, were forbidden full participation in the country's democracy. Whether it was the prohibition on voting or being forbidden to serve on a jury, obtain a loan, or attend public schools, for decades Black Americans were institutionally forbidden from exercising the rights that are foundational to American exceptionalism. Black Americans were tax-paying citizens who were overtly and covertly prohibited from exercising the rights that the constitution afforded. The historical precedent for humiliation based on skin color meant that Black Americans were institutionally and systematically forced to endure state-sanctioned humiliation.

While the federal complicity that historically supported these legal structures would eventually end with the Montgomery Bus Boycott and Rosa Parks' exhaustion with the humiliation of segregated busing (Shultziner, 2013), the consequences of the long-standing practice of institutional racism left a legacy that endures. This impact manifests itself societally in many ways; however, none is greater or more powerful than racism's effect on our nation's public schools (Frankenburg & Orfield, 2012).

Since the landmark *Brown v. Board of Education* (1954) decision, public education has been perceived as an equitable space and Black children were no longer constitutionally prohibited from attending public schools (Ackerman, 2014). Chief Justice Warren claimed as much when he stated, "Separating the races is usually interpreted as denoting the inferiority of the Negro group. A sense of inferiority affects the motivation of a child to learn," which "generates a feeling of inferiority as to their status in the community that may affect their hearts and minds in a way unlikely ever to be undone" (Brown v. Board of Education, 1954, p. 494). Nevertheless, despite this landmark decision, institutionalized humiliation remains a central aspect of public school culture. While equitable access to public schools was necessary to minimize its impact, it is insufficient to counteract the ways in which institutional discrimination can manifest. This was one of the central limitations of *Brown*. While the institutional humiliation of between-school segregation had ended, the phenomenon of within-school segregation would simply fill its place, creating the basis for one of the most talked-about issues in public education today: the achievement gap.

Institutional Racial Humiliation in K–12 Schools

The achievement gap most frequently refers to the disparity between racial groups in performance on standardized tests. Born of the *No Child Left Behind* era, the achievement gap is used to highlight performance differences between students or schools. While intended to magnify the *treatment* (emphasis mine) between racial groups of students within a school, the achievement gap instead is frequently portrayed as a Black/White binary indicator of the cognitive ability of students. The result of this framing, absent the historical context for differential treatment, reinforces the deficit thinking (Valencia, 2010) and perceptions of Black intellectual deficits that pervade educational culture. The performance of White students is considered normal, while the performance of Black students is considered aberrant, under the meritocratic premise that "all things are equal." Thus, the inappropriate framing of the achievement gap becomes the discursive application of "institutionalized humiliation" (Ackerman, 2014, p. 13) in an institutionally racist context.

Achievement gap discourse blames children for their academic results without consideration of the efforts of the schools (Carey, 2014; Cobb & Russell, 2014). The achievement gap concept assumes that all students, regardless of race, are afforded an equivalent experience and receive different academic results despite that fair treatment. Research repeatedly verifies that this has never been true (Cobb & Russell, 2014).

The "gap" is in access to quality learning opportunities, not in achieve-ment. Nonetheless, the term "achievement gap" remains a central principle in America's public schools, accomplishing the ultimate goal of humiliating the target. Through its repeated use, the achievement gap mantra encourages belief in a level playing field and suggests that Black students' poor academic outcomes make them worthy of humiliation.

The psychic cost of use of this inaccurate phrase affects Black stu-dents even when they are academically prepared and provided access to quality learning experiences. Known as stereotype threat, this phe-nomenon affects the performance of Black students in academic con-texts when they fixate on avoiding the humiliating stereotype of Black underperformance (Inzlicht & Schmader, 2012; Steele, 2011). When focused on proving that Black intelligence is equal to that of any other group, the attention dedicated to disprove the stereotype ironically leads students to confirm the very behavior that they were trying to avoid. Black students, in an effort to prove their intelligence, become overwhelmed by the stigma of failure, such that the pre-*Brown* legacy still affects "hearts and minds (of all students) in a way unlikely ever to be undone" (Brown v. Board of Education, 1954, p. 494).

Cultural Humiliation

Finally, Griffin (1991) stated that cultural racism "defines the culture of one group as superior to that of any other group" (p. 151). Incor-porating elements from individual and institutional racism, cultural racism relies upon popular culture as its vehicle and justification to enact racial humiliation. Born out of the early days of "television, radio, newsprint, film, and theater" (Griffin, 1991, p. 151), mass media have historically been deployed as a prominent, pervasive tool of racial humiliation. Relying on the use of exaggerated caricatures of Black Americans, cultural racism dehumanizes Black Americans by normal-izing stereotypes.

Whether in plays or novels, advertisements, magazines, movies, or television shows, subhuman depictions of Black Americans have dominated popular culture for decades. Historical characters such as Zip Coon, Uncle Tom, Buck, and Pickaninny (Taylor & Austeen, 2012) all depicted Black men as lazy, uneducated, childish, animalistic, and worthy of fear. Black women, not immune to this type of stereotyping, were depicted as either a subservient, maternal, and asexual Mammy, or a hypersexual, hedonistic Jezebel (Ladson-Billings, 2009). These characters were portrayed in a manner that lampooned and mocked Black Americans.

For those who did not have regular exposure to Black Americans, these subhuman depictions soon became "representative" of the Black community. Whether it was White actors like Thomas Rice or Al Jolson performing in blackface, or Black actors like Bert Williams, Dewey "Pigmeat" Markham, Bill "Bojangles" Robinson, and Hattie McDaniel performing as exaggerated caricatures of their racial brethren, these performances gave movie-going audiences the psychological pleasure of observing racial humiliation firsthand. Moreover, these caricatures were oblivious to the humiliating context of their behaviors. This blind spot, similar to Carlton's in *The Fresh Prince of Bel Air*, prevented the caricatures from disassociating from their humiliation. Popular culture's repeated, unchallenged subhuman depictions cemented the American cultural rationalization for Black humiliation.

These chronic, negative depictions led to dire consequences that can be perceived even today. Research repeatedly confirms that many Americans maintain implicit assumptions and dehumanizing stereotypes about Black Americans similar to those historically presented in popular culture (Asim, 2007; Park et al., 2015; Steele, 2011). The stereotypical belief that Black Americans are inherently lazy, subservient, violent, and/or unintelligent persist. The broad application and acceptance of these stereotypes accomplish the singular purpose of dehumanization. Even in instances when Black Americans are considered exceptional, the rationalization for such talents is directly and at times explicitly associated with our inhumanity.

Research also confirms that many Americans consider Black American talents to be otherworldly when compared to those of other Americans (Trawalter & Hoffman, 2015). These talents or abilities include clairvoyance, superhuman strength, or God-like qualities (Hoffman, 2014); this form of supernatural dehumanization is most commonly applied to Black celebrities. Websites, blogs, social media, television outlets, or magazines regularly portray Black American celebrities as superhuman beings. Whether it's Beyoncé, Serena Williams, Stephen Curry, LeBron James, or Barack Obama, mass media are filled with images and articles that define these individuals' unique talents as "out of this world."

Certainly, this perception of superhumanness has much to do with America's infatuation with celebrity; nonetheless, supernatural beliefs about the vocal, physical, or oratory capacities of Black American celebrities are normalized. When references are made to Black American celebrities, supernatural comparisons often follow, leading many to believe these exaggerated depictions are not only true but must be exclusively applied to one race.

While the superhuman stereotypes of Black Americans celebrities are commonplace, their application to noncelebrities is equally pervasive. Although from a distance these stereotypes might appear to provide psychological benefits to Black Americans who are noncelebrities, upon closer inspection it is apparent that these superhuman stereotypes are equally as dehumanizing. For example, scholars have found that the consequence of this superhuman stereotype has led people of all races to believe that Black Americans are less susceptible to pain than White Americans (Forgiarini, M., Gallucci, M., & Maravita, 2011; Silverstein, 2013; Trawalter & Hoffman, 2016). It is posited that the real world implications of this stereotype is what leads to disparate rates of school discipline and ultimately results in Black Americans being treated more harshly by the criminal justice system (Silverstein, 2013).

The consequence of individuals accepting the legitimacy of these superhuman stereotypes presents a challenge for the perspective taking of the injustice that Black Americans routinely encounter. Silverstein (2013) has termed this phenomenon the racial empathy gap. Therefore the belief that Black Americans are somehow different even when it appears to work to our advantage can also cut against us like a double edge sword.

Consider the relatives of the victims massacred at the Mother Emanuel African Methodist and Episcopal Church in Charleston, South Carolina in 2015. Here, a self-professed racist committed the ultimate atrocity of murdering nine complete strangers in their place of worship. First welcomed as a guest by the parishioners during their weekly Bible study, the murderer waited until those in attendance began to pray before executing nine of the 12 churchgoers in attendance. Using the Confederate Flag as justification for racial humiliation, the murderer confessed committing this heinous act in hopes of starting a broader "race war."

The inhumanity and outright cruelty of this massacre was obvious. No person or group, regardless of their religion, deserves such treatment. Everyone, regardless of race, could understand what it might feel like to be the victim of such a horrendous crime for doing nothing other than praying in one's house of worship. The act was abominable and the murderer was justified in receiving the harshest punishment our judicial system offers.

Yet once the killer was arraigned, the media (both traditional and social) shifted its focus to the God-like choice of *some* (emphasis mine) family members to forgive him (Berman, 2015; Wear, 2015). The media reported the victims' relatives' uncanny ability to maintain their faith and dignity when confronting the man who deployed the ultimate form of racial humiliation. These relatives were rightfully devastated, yet popular culture diminished their collective humanity by implying that their God-like ability to forgive somehow shielded them from the unspeakable pain of having a relative murdered. These average church-going individuals went from anonymous to superhuman in an instant. They did so while American society normalized the sub-human/superhuman stereotype of Black Americans. They were grieving and responding to this unbelievable tragedy in a way that their faith instructed, yet before long, the victims' families will sit alongside a myriad of superhuman Black Americans in our history books. Their God-like ability to forgive a heinous killer will likely be mythologized with time, adding to the litany of implicit lessons on Black superhumanization that are routinely taught to our nation's children.

Cultural Humiliation in the K–12 Curriculum

In the K–12 educational context, cultural racism shows up most prominently via the curriculum. Specifically, this is observed via the use of racially insensitive literature that routinely employed exaggerated stereotypes to construct the language and persona of Black characters (Asim, 2007). Here, as in popular culture, Black Americans are frequently presented as superhuman or subhuman, rendering Black normality practically invisible. This shortsighted pairing of stereotypes rarely affords students the opportunity to view Black Americans as fully human. This reality is not because we do not exist in history but, as Ellison (1952) suggests, because "people refuse to see (us)" (p. 1). This absence sends an important message to students of all races. If Black Americans are not subhuman male figures, such as Jim from *The Adventures of Huckleberry Finn*, Bigger Thomas from *Native Son*, or Tom Robinson from *To Kill a Mockingbird*, then we must be the exceptional Thurgood Marshall, Martin Luther King, Frederick Douglas, W. E. B. Dubois, or Jackie Robinson. If we are not the subhuman Mammy or Jezebel, then we must be the phenomenal Rosa Parks, Harriett Tubman, Sojourner Truth, or Maya Angelou. Black Americans in the curriculum must be divinely extraordinary or subservient buffoons. There is no in-between.

The consequence of the lack of cultural complexity in the curriculum reinforces the images that dominate popular culture. As a result, Black Americans must contend with annual discussions on the inappropriateness of White students dressing up as their favorite Black entertainers for Halloween or, worse yet, routine examples of students using the anti-Black racial slur that has come to define Black humiliation. Confused by negative responses, these students engage in these acts under the assumption that their behavior and the subsequent humiliation of Black Americans is normal, because this is what they learned in school. Thus, covering one's face in brown make-up and dressing as an exaggerated depiction of Lil Wayne, Beyoncé, or Serena Williams for Halloween at a school event seems justifiable because Black Americans are presented as exceptional or worthy of mockery. Furthermore, using the most racially loaded slur in the English language in school classrooms or hallways, or standing alongside five of your closest friends to spell out a derivative of that slur on your t-shirts seems normal (Carrero, 2016), because cultural humiliation is central to the hidden curriculum of schools (Giroux & Penna, 1979).

Moreover, when an educational leader—especially one who is Black—challenges these practices, he is frequently regarded as being overly concerned with political correctness. The phrase "it's a part of history," perceived as a justifiable defense, sends the clear signal that the need to preserve one's desire to humiliate and dehumanize is of greater importance than protecting Black America's right to live free from racial humiliation. Therefore, overly sensitive individuals should simply calm down, be quiet, "stay in their place," and let students have their moment of fun. Politically correct culture is the problem, not the dehumanizing actors.

Far too many educators teach our nation's children that Black Americans only exist as a dehumanizing binary (subhuman and super-human), both of which are equally deserving of degradation. Whether the hidden curricular application of racial humiliation is enacted con-sciously or subconsciously is irrelevant: The effect is the same. Students learn that all Black Americans are superhuman or subhuman creatures deserving of humiliation and unworthy of compassion. Cultural racism and the accompanying tactic of racial humiliation are inescapable, because to so many they are normal and foundational to our collective racial habits. This can be suffocating, especially for Black leaders. The presence of this cultural dynamic encourages Black Americans to hope for a time when they can take a moment to escape and just breathe.

The Django Fantasy

In 2014, director Quentin Tarantino released the wildly successful spaghetti western, *Django Unchained*. Starring Jamie Foxx, Leonardo DiCaprio, Christoph Waltz, and Kerry Washington, the film tells the story of a freed slave in the antebellum South searching for his long-lost love. The title character, Django, is offered help in finding his wife from the dentist-turned-bounty hunter, King Shultz, if he agrees to partner with him in arresting or killing wanted outlaws. For Django, the relationship seemed to be a win all the way around: He is granted his freedom, given an opportunity to find his wife, and afforded a chance to seek vengeance against whomever he chooses.

The plot represents the perfect revenge fantasy, as a formerly enslaved character is given the authority to kill wanted criminals without fear of retribution. What's more, his new profession gives Django the opportunity to kill his former overseers, who caused him and his lost wife physical and psychological harm. *Django Unchained* upends the historical dynamic of racial humiliation. Django is granted repeated opportunities to whip, torture, and dehumanize his oppressors and, while violent, his acts are always presented as justified. In this fictional world, a Black man is the perpetrator of humiliation against White targets, while enslaved Africans play the role of witnesses.

After a winter of killing countless wanted criminals, taking righteous pleasure in each and every death, King Shultz discovers that Django's wife, Broomhilda, is enslaved on a plantation famed for forcing the enslaved to fight to the death. This horrendous sport, dubbed "Mandingo fights," is likened to the animal fighting that occurs in the shadows of society today. The plantation owner, Calvin Candie, is justified in promoting this heinous sport by his belief that the enslaved are animalistic and subhuman, relying upon the pseudosciences of eugenics and phrenology. Candie believes the brains of most of the enslaved Blacks predispose them to enduring great pain and being more submissive than White Americans. However, Candie is quick to assert that he does not believe that this applies to all enslaved Blacks. He is certain about 1 in 10,000 are exceptional, a "level above bright, above talented, above loyal," and that Django is one of these unique individuals.

As a free man, Django adopts a persona that only certain White characters are allowed utterly transcending his race. He rides a horse, carries a gun, dresses in new clothes, and demands respect from everyone he encounters. Those who meet him are utterly amazed. From their perspective, Black men were either incapable of acting as he did or were not afforded the permissions to do so. Observing a Black man behave with Django's dignity was analogous to seeing an alien, because

Django did not consider himself to be vulnerable at a time in history where the vulnerability of Black Americans was magnified. Django, as Dubois (1903/1994) might have noted, lived beyond the veil of race, and forced the world to see him the way he saw himself, rather than the other way around.

One of the most memorable scenes of the film the first meeting of Django and Candie's lead "House Negro," Stephen. Prior to meeting Django, Stephen considered himself to be exceptional. As Candie's close friend and favorite, Stephen believed himself to be special because he was allowed to do things that the plantation's other enslaved were not. Upon seeing Django, he stood with mouth agape, confused that a Black man was doing things he was not allowed to do. Staring, Stephen slowly tilted his head, perplexed that he was seeing a Black man on a horse. Finally, he asked, "Why is *he* on this horse?" Stephen was incensed when Candie informed him that Django was a free man who would stay in the "big house" and be treated like the other Whites on the plantation. Not only was Stephen suffering from the cognitive dissonance of seeing a Black man do things that he could not, he was required to cater to Django as to a White. Moreover, throughout the rest of the film, Stephen stops at nothing to see Django fail, believing it to be his responsibility to put Django in his place and prove that he is unremarkable.

Nevertheless, throughout the film's entire two hours and forty-five minutes, Django finds ways to embody the exceptionalism that Candie discovered in him. In every scene, Django finds a way to maintain his dignity, define how he wants to be viewed, and refuse to submit to any other characters. Even when Django is captured and the upended racial order appears to be on the brink of being restored, he escapes and exercises his newfound agency on a world that has caused him so much pain. Django proves to be exceptional and this mindset allows him to save his wife and live happily ever after.

Despite the many controversies that surrounded the release of this film, *Django Unchained* represented a fantasy shared by many Black Americans: confronting discourtesies, indignities and attempts at dehumanization without reprisal while defining the world's perceptions of what it meant to be Black would be the epitome of satisfaction. Living in a world where Black authority is not only considered normal but earns the same level of respect as any other group would be truly validating. However, much like the title of this section, this is nothing more than fantasy. History repeatedly verifies that when Black Americans stand up to racial humiliation, they risk their lives. Standing up against injustice is, truly, a revolutionary act. Historically, this has been confirmed through the public lynchings of countless ancestors such as Emmitt Till and the assassinations of historically prominent figures, including Medgar Evers and Martin Luther King Jr. Today, we think of Trayvon Martin, Jordan Davis, Eric Garner, and Sandra Bland. These individuals stood up for their dignity in the face of racial humiliation and it cost them their lives. They refused to "stay in their place" and directly confronted dehumanization. Despite the clear injustices that surrounded their murders, the message is clear: Black Americans who stand up to racial humiliation take a life-threatening risk.

I learned this harsh reality firsthand as an undergraduate student at Howard University. It was here that my reality was upended after the slaying of a fellow Howardite: Prince Jones. As brilliantly documented by another classmate of mine, Ta-nehisi Coates (2001; 2009; 2015), Jones was on his way from Prince George's County in Maryland to Arlington, Virginia to visit his fiancée, when a plainclothes police officer saw him and believed he "fit the description" of a drug dealer. The officer followed Jones for 15 miles through three jurisdictions, including the District of Columbia and two states. According to police accounts, when Jones arrived in Arlington, he realized he was being followed and pulled into a driveway of a home not far from his fiancée's residence. Concerned, Jones exited his car and confronted the officer. The officer contends that he identified himself by drawing his gun instead of showing his badge to indicate that he was a police officer (Cherkis & Diaz, 2000). Upon seeing the weapon, and likely in disbelief of the plainclothes officer's claim, Jones got back in his car, backed out of the driveway, and attempted to ram the officer. The officer, now on the defensive, raised his weapon and fired at Jones sixteen times, hitting him five times in the back (Cherkis & Diaz, 2000).

By all accounts, Jones lived his life well. Like me, he entered Howard as a suburban kid who had been among the one percent of Black students in his K–12 school. Upon graduation, he planned to be commissioned as an officer in the United States Navy and then become a radiologist like his mother (Cherkis & Diaz, 2000). Like most of my classmates, Jones made the right decisions, played by the rules, stayed out of trouble, and got a good education. Nonetheless, he was killed because of his association with the superhuman stereotypes of Blackness. In a theme reflected in similar news stories, the officer bore no criminal responsibility for Jones's death. Eventually, the officer proceeded with his life. However, Jones and the members of his family could not.

Although I did not know Jones personally, I was very familiar with his story. His death sent shockwaves through the Howard University community, who found the death of a classmate at the hands of a police officer incomprehensible. What's more, it was unbelievable that such a tragedy could occur with no claim of responsibility by the police. This was not supposed to happen to one of us, because as Howard students we knew we were destined to extend our university's tradition of Black excellence.

With knowledge of the incredible contributions of our famous alumni, we knew that we could accomplish anything because our time at Howard University allowed us to live beyond the veil of race and achieve our self-conscious adulthood (Dubois, 1903/1994). Therefore, if we so chose, we knew that we could change the course of history. We were the legacy of the incredible minds that successfully argued to overturn segregation. We were the decedents of the first Black American to become a Supreme Court Justice and the first Black woman to practice law. A Howard graduate who became the first Black American governor and another was the first Black American to win the Nobel Peace Prize. As the metaphorical sons and daughters of this legacy, clenched fists raised proudly in the air, we knew that we were different. We were young, gifted, and Black. We were accepted by that institution because we were "exceptional" and we knew that we were that "one in 10,000." Therefore, a tragedy like this was not supposed to happen to one of us. And yet it did. Despite the psychic armor provided by

Howard University, Jones's killing reminded us that, once we left the safe confines of our Northwest Washington DC campus, we could still "fit the description," be unjustly killed, and then be blamed for our own deaths (Imani, 2016). Our truth did not matter.

Although most of my classmates did not share my suburban, California accent, in some ways we were all as naïve as Carlton. We did not run around campus wearing bow ties and sweaters over our collared shirts, or dance awkwardly to the music of Tom Jones, but we did in a sense think that we were above it all. While many of us would likely never admit it, we were just like Carlton driving to Palm Springs, believing that our obvious exceptionality and the psychic armor that our Howard University education provided would keep us safe. Deep down we believed we were special, invincible, and immune to humiliation—yet in truth we were living a *Django*-like fantasy because we could not transcend race. In an era dominated by names like Trayvon Martin, Jordan Davis, Philando Castile, Renisha McBride, and Sandra Bland, we knew Prince Jones (Coates, 2015).

That incomprehensible tragedy forced us to realize that, despite our education and impending professional status, our racial identity would remain a dominant aspect of our personal and professional lives. On campus, we defined our identities and determined how the world saw us, yet our classmate's homicide reminded us that the outside world would force us to face our own double consciousness. While Dubois (1903) asked the profound and ever-relevant question, "How does it feel to be a problem?," we were also contending with the more immediate Gatesian (1997) question: "How does it feel to be a paradox?" While we knew we were exceptional, we realized that society demanded that we acquiesce and conform to a more palatable, less aggressive, and somewhat passive version of our racial identity—although doing so would not ensure that we would be seen as human and thereby avoid being profiled. We had to accept that, despite our assumed exceptionality, attempts at racial humiliation could occur by anyone at any time, placing our psyches somewhere between that of Carlton Banks and Django.

Leading in Between

As I have reflected on my attempts to address inequality in all its forms, and the emotional labor (Hochschild, 2012) that I have contended with as a result, I have often felt that my leadership identity is somewhere between Carlton Banks and Django. While both are impractical fictional portrayals, they do in a way represent my double consciousness and working identity in a field that has a history of inequitable treatment towards children who share my racial heritage. I am always caught in the humiliating double bind of feeling *too Black* and *not Black enough*.

While my purpose in educational leadership is to bring about change and address educational injustice for all students, particularly those who have been historically marginalized, it is clear that some individuals would prefer that I remain quiet, content, and grateful for my professional ascendancy despite the presence of racial injustice. Instead of supporting me in attending to the indignity and racial humiliation that disproportionately affects children who look like me, some would rather simply enjoy the benefits of my presence and all of the plausible deniability that that my racial identity creates, leaving me feeling like nothing more than a "poorly utilized token" (Cose, 1994, p. 46).

While bearing witness to this dilemma, my impatient and critical identity wants to unleash my authority, making whatever changes are necessary and disregarding the consequences. However, the pragmatic nature of leadership keeps me mindful that behaving in such a reckless fashion carries a political and social cost that might prevent me from supporting the students who need me most. Consequently, leading for educational equity while Black is among the most challenging of educational leadership tasks, because we are trying to improve the lives of children who look like us while constantly negotiating the tension between the unapologetically Black people we are and the acceptably Black individuals that many want us to be.

References

Ackerman, B. (2014). *We the people: The civil rights revolution (Vol. 3)*. Cambridge, MA: Belknap Press.

Allen, Q. (2010). Racial microaggressions: The schooling experiences of Black middle-class males in Arizona's secondary schools. *Journal of African American Males in Education, 1*(2), 125–143.

Asim, J. (2007). *The N word: Who can say it, who shouldn't, and why*. New York, NY: Houghton Mifflin Harcourt.

Berman, J. (2015, June 19). 'I forgive you.' Relatives of Charleston church shooting victims address Dylann Roof. *The Washington Post*. Retrieved from https://www.washingtonpost.com/news/post-nation/wp/2015/06/19/i-forgive-you-relatives-of-charleston-church-victims-address-dylann-roof/?utm_term=.770d298554a3

Borowitz, S. (Writer), Borowitz, A. (Writer), & Melman, J. (Director). (1990). Mistaken identity [Television series episode]. In S. Borowitz, & A. Borowitz (Producer), *The Fresh Prince of Bel Air*. Los Angeles, CA: National Broadcasting Company.

Brown, B. (2012). *Daring greatly: How the courage to be vulnerable transforms the way we live, love, parent, and lead*. London: Avery.

Brown v. Board of Education, 347 U.S. 483 (1954).

Browder v. Gayle, 352 U.S. 903 (1956).

Carey, R. L. (2014). A cultural analysis of the achievement gap discourse challenging the language and labels used in the work of school reform. *Urban Education, 49*(4), 440–468.

Carrero, J. (2016, January 25). Phoenix students photographed spelling racial slur with t-shirts. *NBC News*. Retrieved from http://www.nbcnews.com/news/us-news/phoenix-students-photographed-spelling-racial-slur-t-shirts-n503711

Cherkis, J., & Diaz, K. (2000, September 22). Black victim, black cop, black county. *Washington City Paper*. Retrieved from http://www.washingtoncitypaper.com/articles/20399/black-victim-black-cop-black-county/

Coates, T. N. (2001). Black and Blue: Why does America's richest black suburb have some of the country's most brutal cops? *Washington Monthly, 33*(6), 25–30. Retrieved from http://www.washingtonmonthly.com/features/2001/0106.coates.html

Coates, T. N. (2015). *Between the world and me*. New York, NY: Spiegel & Grau.

Cobb, F., & Russell, N. M. (2014). Meritocracy or complexity: Problematizing racial disparities in mathematics assessment within the context of curricular structures, practices, and discourse. *Journal of Education Policy 30*(5), 631–649.

Christian, C. M., & Bennett, S. (1998). *Black Saga: The African American experience: A chronology*. New York, NY: Basic Civitas Books.

Cobb, F., (2012). *It's About Access: How the Curricular System and Unequal Learning Opportunities Predict The Racial Test Score Gap in Mathematics* (Doctoral dissertation, University of Denver. Retrieved from http://digitalcommons.du.edu/cgi/viewcontent.cgi?article=1783&context=etd

Cose, E. (1993). *The rage of a privileged class: Why are middle-class Blacks angry? Why should America care.* New York, NY: Harper Perennial.

Darley, J., & Latane, B. (1968). When will people help in a crisis? *Psychology Today, 2*(54), 70–71.

DuBois, W. E. B. (1994). *The souls of Black folk.* New York, NY: Dover Publications. (Original Work published 1903.)

Fanon, F. (1967). *Black skin, white masks: The experiences of a black man in a white world.* New York, NY: Grove Press.

Fernández, S., Saguy, T., & Halperin, E. (2015). The paradox of humiliation: The acceptance of an unjust devaluation of the self. *Personality and Social Psychology Bulletin, 41*(7), 976–988. doi:0146167215586195.

Fisk, C. L. (2001). Humiliation at work. *William and Mary Journal of Women and the Law, 8*(1), 73–95.

Fiske, S. T. (2013). Varieties of (de) humanization: Divided by competition and status. In S. J. Gervais (Ed.), *Objectification and (de) humanization* (pp. 53–71). 60th Nebraska Symposium on Motivation: Springer. doi:10.1007/978-1-4614-6959-9_3

Frankenberg, E., & Orfield, G. (2012). *The resegregation of suburban schools: A hidden crisis in American education.* Cambridge, MA: Harvard Education Press.

Gates, H. L., Jr. (1995, October 23). Thirteen ways of looking at a Black man. *The New Yorker.* Retrieved from http://www.newyorker.com/magazine/1995/10/23/thirteen-ways-of-looking-at-a-black-man

Giroux, H. A., & Penna, A. N. (1979). Social education in the classroom: the dynamics of the hidden curriculum. *Theory & Research in Social Education, 7*(1), 21–42.

Gregory, A., Skiba, R. J., & Noguera, P. A. (2010). The achievement gap and the discipline gap two sides of the same coin? *Educational Researcher, 39*(1), 59–68.

Griffin, J. T. (1991). Racism and humiliation in the African-American community. *The journal of primary prevention, 12*(2), 149–167.

Hanson, J. D., & Hanson, K. (2006). The blame frame: Justifying (racial) injustice in America. *Harvard Civil Rights-Civil Liberties Law Review, 41*, 08–47.

Hartling, L. M., Lindner, E., Spalthoff, U., & Britton, M. (2013). Humiliation: A nuclear bomb of emotions? *Psicologia Politica, 46*, 55–76.

Humiliate [Def. 1]. (n.d.). In *Merriam Webster Online,* Retrieved January 8, 2016, from http://www.merriam-webster.com/dictionary/humiliate

Imani, Z. [ZellieImani]. (2016, July 12). *White supremacy will kill you, and then blame you for your own death.* #AltonSterling #PhilandoCastile [Tweet]. Retrieved from https://twitter.com/zellieimani/status/752838214826790912

Inzlicht, M., & Schmader, T. (2012). *Stereotype threat: Theory, process, and application.* New York, NY: Oxford University Press.

King M. L., Jr. (1964). *Nobel Lecture.* Retrieved from http://www.nobelprize.org/nobel_prizes/peace/laureates/1964/king-lecture.html

Klein, D. C. (1991). The humiliation dynamic: An overview. *Journal of Primary Prevention, 12*(2), 93–121.

Kohli, R., & Solórzano, D. G. (2012). Teachers, please learn our names!: Racial micro-aggressions and the K–12 classroom. *Race Ethnicity and Education, 15*(4), 441–462.

Ladson-Billings, G. (2009). "Who you callin' nappy-headed?" A critical race theory look at the construction of Black women. *Race Ethnicity and Education, 12*(1), 87–99.

Ledesma, M. C. & Solorzano, D. G. (2013). Naming their pain: How everyday racial microaggressions impact students and teachers. In D. J. Carter Andrews & F. Tuitt (Eds.), *Contesting the myth of a "post-racial" era: the continued significance of race in U.S. education* (pp.112–127). New York, NY: Peter Lang.

Lerner, M. L. (1980), *The belief in a just world: A fundamental delusion.* New York, NY: Plenum Press.

Linder, E. (2009). *Emotion and conflict: How human rights can dignify emotion and help us wage good conflict.* Westport, CT: Greenwood Publishing Group.

Miller, W. I. (1993). *Humiliation: And other essays on honor, social discomfort, and violence.* Ithaca, NY: Cornell University Press.

Morris, E. W., & Perry, B. L. (2016). The punishment gap: School suspension and racial disparities in achievement. *Social Problems, 63*(1), 68–86.

Omi, M., & Winant, H. (2014). *Racial formation in the United States.* New York, NY: Routledge.

Okonofua, J. A., & Eberhardt, J. L. (2015). Two strikes race and the disciplining of young students. *Psychological science, 26*(5), 617–624.

Otten, M., & Jonas, K. J. (2014). Humiliation as an intense emotional experience: Evidence from the electro-encephalogram. *Social Neuroscience, 9*(1), 23–35.

Park, J. Z., Martinez, B. C., Cobb, R., Park, J. J., & Wong, E. R. (2015). Exceptional out-group stereotypes and White racial inequality attitudes toward Asian Americans. *Social Psychology Quarterly, 78*(4), 399–411.

Parks, R., & Haskins, J. (1992). *Rosa Parks: My story.* London: Puffin Books.

Pierce, C. I. (1970). Offensive mechanisms. In F. Barbour (Ed.), *The Black seventies* (pp. 265–282). Boston, MA: Porter Sargent.

Salmivalli, C. (2010). Bullying and the peer group: A review. *Aggression and violent behavior, 15*(2), 112–120.

Shultziner, D. (2013). The social-psychological origins of the Montgomery bus boycott: Social interaction and humiliation in the emergence of social movements. *Mobilization: An International Quarterly, 18*(2), 117–142.

Skiba, R. J., Michael, R. S., Nardo, A. C., & Peterson, R. L. (2002). The color of discipline: Sources of racial and gender disproportionality in school punishment. *The Urban Review, 34*(4), 317–342.

Skiba, R. J., Horner, R. H., Chung, C. G., Karega Rausch, M., May, S. L., & Tobin, T. (2011). Race is not neutral: A national investigation of African American and Latino disproportionality in school discipline. *School Psychology Review, 40*(1), 85.

Smith, E. J., & Harper, S. R. (2015). *Disproportionate impact of K–12 school suspension and expulsion on Black students in southern states.* Retrieved from University of

Pennsylvania, Center for the Study of Race and Equity in Education website: http://www.gse.upenn.edu/equity/SouthernStates

Solorzano, D., Ceja, M., & Yosso, T. (2000). Critical race theory, racial microaggressions, and campus racial climate: The experiences of African American college students. *Journal of Negro Education, 69,* (1)60–73.

Steele, C. (2011). *Whistling Vivaldi: How stereotypes affect us and what we can do (issues of our time).* New York, NY: WW Norton & Company.

Sue, D. W. (2010). *Microaggressions in everyday life: Race, gender, and sexual orientation.* Hoboken, NJ: John Wiley & Sons.

Sue, D. W., Capodilupo, C. M., Torino, G. C., Bucceri, J. M., Holder, A., Nadal, K. L., Esquilin, M. (2007). Racial microaggressions in everyday life: Implications for clinical practice. *American Psychologist, 62*(4), 271.

Sue, D. W., Capodilupo, C. M., & Holder, A. (2008). Racial microaggressions in the life experience of Black Americans. *Professional Psychology: Research and Practice, 39*(3), 329.

Sullivan, S. (2006). *Revealing whiteness: The unconscious habits of racial privilege.* Bloomington, IN: Indiana University Press.

Takahashi, H., Kato, M., Matsuura, M., Mobbs, D., Suhara, T., & Okubo, Y. (2009). When your gain is my pain and your pain is my gain: Neural correlates of envy and schadenfreude. *Science, 323*(5916), 937–939.

Taylor, Y., & Austen, J. (2012). *Darkest America: Black minstrelsy from slavery to hip-hop.* New York, NY: WW Norton & Company.

Torres, W. J., & Bergner, R. M. (2010). Humiliation: Its nature and consequences. *Journal of the American Academy of Psychiatry and the Law Online, 38*(2), 195–204.

Trawalter, S., & Hoffman, K. M. (2016). Got pain? Racial Bias in perceptions of pain. *Social and Personality Psychology Compass, 9*(3), 146–157.

Valencia, R. R. (2010). *Dismantling contemporary deficit thinking: Educational thought and practice.* New York, NY: Routledge.

Wear, M. (2015, June 24). Stop Explaining Away Black Christian Forgiveness. *Christianity Today.* Retrieved from http://www.christianitytoday.com/ct/2015/june-webonly/stop-explaining-away-black-christian-forgiveness.html

Woodson, C. G. (2010). *The mis-education of the negro.* USA: Seven Treasures Publications. (Original work published in 1933).

Wright, A. C. (2015). Teachers' Perceptions of Students' Disruptive Behavior: The Effect of Racial Congruence and Consequences for School Suspension. *Unpublished manuscript. Santa Barbara, CA: University of California Department of Economics. Available from http://www. econ. ucsb. edu/jobmarket/Wright,% 20Adam*

Zinn, H. (2016). *A people's history of the United States.* New York, NY: HarperPerennial.

Zuberi, T. (2008). Deracializing social statistics: Problems in the quantification of race. In T. Zuberi, & E. Bonilla-Silva (Eds.), *White logic, white methods: racism and methodology* (pp. 127–136). Lanham, MD: Rowman & Littlefield.

Chapter 3

The Miseducation of the Black Leader

Philosophers have long conceded, however, that every man has two educations: the one which is given to him and the one which he gives to himself. Of the two kinds, the latter is by far more desirable.

—*Woodson, 1933/2010, p. 67*

Presumption of Guilt

Upon graduating from Howard University, the need to confront my double consciousness and vulnerability was foremost in my mind. With two bachelor's degrees in hand, it was clear that I had defied the odds and shed the stereotypical assumptions of what it meant to be a Black male. Nonetheless, I was hyperaware that, despite these credentials, the assumption of criminality was never far.

I was coming off an incredible student teaching experience at the District of Columbia Public Schools (D.C.P.S.) magnet school, School Without Walls, located on the campus of the George Washington

University. Teaching there gave me an opportunity to use all the instructional skills and talents I had acquired. I absolutely loved teaching high school social studies to my students and realized that the field of education was a natural fit for me. That experience truly illustrated to me how much of a difference one person could make, especially when that person loves what he does.

After completing that experience, I believed my career path was set: I was going to teach social studies, coach baseball, and have a wonderful career. However, my advisor at Howard was quick to remind me of the competitive nature of job-hunting. He noted that my placement at the School Without Walls was a direct result of that difficulty, and told me that if this was something I truly wanted to do, I would be wise to bolster my resume and obtain a master's degree before seeking a job.

Pursuing graduate studies at George Washington University seemed like a good idea. After six months of experience on the campus, I was accustomed to the culture and appreciated the wonderful opportunities the downtown university offered. While attending college at a predominantly White university was going to bring back the stress of hypervisibility as the only Black male in many of my courses, I believed that it would not affect me too much. I would be okay because I was in a majority Black city and very likely could blend in most places I went.

At the time, the School of Education and Human Development was developing a brand-new master's degree program in curriculum and instruction that focused on Bilingual Special Education. This program would prepare its graduates to meet the social, cultural, and linguistic needs of exceptional students. Upon completion, I would be qualified to obtain certifications in Special Education, Bilingual Education, and English as a Second Language. In addition to my certifications in History and Spanish, this degree would broaden my background and allow me to become the best history teacher I could possibly be. I had found the right university and program, I was in the right city, and I knew I was going to enjoy every minute of my time on that campus.

Once accepted, I learned that the Bilingual Special Education program was different from many of the other master's degree programs at the university in that we rarely had courses that met on the campus

I had come to adore. Instead, we were housed at a public school located a short distance away in the Georgetown neighborhood. While the amenities were not comparable to those of the Foggy Bottom campus, I understood that the Hardy middle school placement served a very practical purpose: During the day, the graduate students would serve as interns, teaching lessons and supporting students under the guidance of an experienced teacher. Once the final bell rang, we would shift our focus to our coursework on educational theory and instructional methods, which contextualized our work with our students. We'd go home no sooner than twelve hours after we arrived, just to wake up the next morning and do it all again.

Being the only Black male in the program created a heavy burden of intense hypervisibility for me. Because I did not want anyone to doubt my seriousness, I followed a strict routine: wake up, eat breakfast, check my plans, and hop in my Mazda pickup to make the short drive over to Georgetown to begin my day. On weekends, I would head to the university library to get caught up on my reading and forthcoming assignments in preparation for the following week. Focused and determined, I rarely deviated from this weekly routine because I felt that being the only Black male in this program meant that I needed to work twice as hard to prove myself.

One Saturday early in my graduate program, a friend asked me to help him move a few large items from his apartment. Knowing how serious I was about my studies, he promised that the move would take no more than an hour, leaving me plenty of time to get back to my studies. Having moved a number of friends, I was doubtful about his promise but agreed to lend a hand. When Saturday morning arrived, I got up early, threw my backpack in my truck, and made the short drive to his house. My friend had kept his promise; he was ready and everything he owned was nearly packed. His two-door car was so crammed with boxes, clothes, and small appliances that there was almost no room for the driver. As I drove past his car, I smiled and shook my head, excited that the job would be short and I'd have plenty of time to study.

The only items remaining to be packed were a mattress, a box spring, and a metal bed frame, all of which would fit easily into the bed of my truck. I thanked him for his preparation and was looking for something to pack, when I heard my truck's alarm going off. Unconcerned, I ignored it, assuming that someone had set it off unintentionally. The only thing in the truck was my backpack with my schoolwork and I could not imagine anyone wanting to take that, so I went back to looking for something to grab. That was when another friend screamed, "Floyd, somebody is breaking into your truck!" In absolute disbelief, I ran to the window and saw two men sprinting down the street with my backpack. My heart fell into my stomach. Furious, I ran down the stairs to see if I could catch them, but it was too late.

I slowly walked to my truck, hoping that my notes were still there. I knew that not having my materials meant that I might fall behind in my studies and, even worse, could confirm the stereotype of the unprepared student. I approached my truck, peered into the broken window and, to my dismay, all I could see were shards of glass where my backpack with all of my books and notes had been. Furious, I balled my fists in complete exasperation and screamed out loud, angry at how foolish this whole situation was going to make me look. I had worked so hard not to fulfill a cultural stereotype, yet in the blink of an eye, two unwitting thieves put me right back in that place.

Feeling helpless and victimized, I shifted my attention to what I could control, which was finding another mode of transportation to the Georgetown campus. Since the distance to the middle school campus was too far to walk and the metro line did not stop near the school, my only remaining transportation option was a taxi. While not terribly skilled at catching cabs, I thought it would not prove much of a problem, as cabs in DC were plentiful.

When Monday morning arrived, I made it a point to get up a bit earlier than usual to make sure that I could get to school well before the bell rang, giving me time to explain my situation to my professor and affirm my commitment to the program. While the story of my robbery was clearly plausible and could have happened to anyone, I was nonetheless fearful appearing to confirm a stereotype. I hoped that by arriving early, I could frame my experience accurately and minimize any rumors that might arise.

I quickly dressed, grabbed my new backpack, and began the walk south from my apartment on 10th Street to the closest busy street, which was Massachusetts Avenue. It was the morning rush hour, and I was relieved to see the street packed with cars and cabs. The incredible volume of traffic led me to believe that my wait for a taxi would be short, allowing me to quickly be on my way to my school. I peered to the southeast and raised my right arm to signal my need for a ride. However, to my surprise, one cab after another drove right past me. Growing a little aggravated, I extended my arm higher and moved closer to the street to make sure that I was seen, but the cabs kept passing me as if I was invisible. Fifteen minutes passed; I might have been a pedestrian. After twenty minutes of waiting, I started to question what I was doing wrong. Was I standing in the wrong place? Had I picked the wrong street? I could not understand what was causing me to repeatedly get passed over for a cab.

After a few minutes of rationalizing, I decided that I must have chosen the wrong street. With a speed limit of 45 miles per hour, the cars on Massachusetts Avenue were driving pretty rapidly. The fact that it would take some effort for a cab driver to slow down during rush hour traffic could easily explain while I was repeatedly being ignored. I certainly did not want to put any drivers in harm's way on a busy street and switching locations might easily remedy the situation. With ample time remaining to get to school early, I hustled over to New York Avenue.

When I got to the new street, I once again peered southeast with my right arm lifted, believing that my luck would be different. However, after a few minutes I realized that little had changed: One cab after another drove past me without the slightest hint of acknowledgement. I saw Black drivers, White drivers, and Middle Eastern drivers, all blazing right past me as if I was invisible. Feeling increasingly humiliated with every cab that passed, I checked my watch and found that half an hour had passed. At this point, I realized that arriving at school early was no longer an option and that the best I could hope for was to arrive before class started. Growing desperate, I extended my right arm even higher, standing on my toes and screaming "Taxi?" as loud as I could.

Still nothing. I jumped up and down, waving my arms, trying everything I could think of to make myself as visible as possible, and yet I was still ignored. It was not long before I started to recognize the faces of drivers who had repeatedly passed me. One by one, they drove right past, not even bothering to turn their heads. After 40 minutes of waiting, my anxiety slowly shifted to rage. It was clear that this had nothing to do with my street selection and everything to do with how I looked. I had done nothing to deserve this treatment and yet it did not matter. Despite my shirt, tie, and preppy collegiate look, I was still viewed as a criminal—no different than the two guys who stole my backpack. The truth did not matter.

Panicked, I started to think of different ways to get to school. The Georgetown location made my only other option the city bus. Trying to do that would have made me even later than if I happened to luck out and catch a cab. Frustrated and paralyzed by anger, I did not know what to do. I wondered if I should call a friend or try another street, but having experienced the same treatment in two different locations I knew I could not guarantee success. Realizing I had few choices, I made the decision to stay on New York Avenue with my arm extended. Soon 40 minutes turned to 50, making it clear that I was going to be late to school. I had never before had trouble catching a cab, but for some reason, on this day of all days, my experience was different. While I'd had my fair share of experiences with racial profiling and knew what it felt like to be pulled over for "fitting the description" and driving while Black, I had never experienced the reality of catching a cab while Black. I waited over an hour, until a cab driver finally stopped to pick me up.

Relieved and utterly humiliated, I got in the back seat told the driver where I was headed. Furious after sixty minutes of waiting, I took a few deep breaths to calm myself. However, when the car started moving I realized that my driver was going to do little to help lower my blood pressure. "Man, that's bullshit," he said. Startled, I grabbed my backpack, worried that he was going to kick me out. He continued, "I saw you standing out there forever. I passed you at least three times but could not pick you up because I had someone else in the car. Every time I came back to try to get you I had to pick up somebody else."

Relieved that I wasn't losing my mind for feeling racially profiled, he continued, "Look at how you're dressed, you've got on a shirt and tie, you're clearly not going to rob anybody. This is bullshit, I hate that this happens to us. I know some of those guys and I'm going to say something, that's some bullshit." Relieved, I thanked him for understanding, telling him again that I appreciated him for picking me up. Nonetheless, he continued muttering under his breath, furious as if he had been the one standing on the sidewalk for an hour. "I hate this racism, man. I hate it. If it's not the police, it's cabs; if it's not cabs, we're being followed around in the store. The shit we go through."

About 10 minutes into the ride, the driver settled down and gave me some advice that I will always remember. He said, "Look man, here is what you do in the future so this never happens to you again. Next time, you need to catch cab, just walk to a hotel, and ask the bellman to call a cab for you. They normally sit outside of the hotels in a line looking to pick up guests and they will never turn the bellman down. The bellman won't know that you're not staying there so don't worry about him. Once you get into the cab, it's against the law for them to kick you out. They have to take you where you want to go once you're in the car. That way you won't ever have to worry about this happening to you again. It's unfair, but so is standing on the corner forever." Shortly thereafter we arrived at the school, where I thanked him again for picking me up, gave him a handsome tip, and hustled into school thirty minutes late.

As I walked into the school, my concerns about confirming a stereotype were compounded. As expected, when I walked into the building my advisors and colleagues looked at me with disappointment. Here I was thirty minutes late and without my assignments or books. I tried to do everything I could to keep from looking foolish but it happened anyway. I told them the story of the theft over the weekend and all I remember seeing were smirks of disbelief. The one thing I feared the most was happening. I had been standing on the sidewalk trying all morning to get to school early, yet those sighs and headshakes left me feeling as if I needed to prove my innocence. When I walked in my building, my guilt was once again assumed. My truth was not to be believed and my facts just did not matter. I had just spent an hour trying to convince cab drivers (many of whom were Black) that I did not deserve to be treated as a criminal and here I was being treated that way again. The people I had come to know were no different than the cab drivers who had not given me the benefit of the doubt, leaving me feeling as vulnerable as when I was standing on that corner. While I had arrived at a place where people knew my character and background, I still felt as if I was being racially profiled.

Race and Place

The practice of racial profiling and the assuming Black American guilt has been culturally accepted in the United States of America for hundreds of years. While immoral and, in most cases, illegal, few Black Americans have not felt the pain of presumptive guilt. Born out of the construct of cultural racism, narrow media representations of Blackness, and the irrational fear of Black violence, the practice of racial profiling is typically defined as any discriminatory treatment imposed solely based upon the race rather than the behavior of an individual (Meehan & Ponder, 2002; Omi & Winant, 2014; Ramirez, McDevitt, & Farrell, 2000). Therefore, instead of differential treatment being justified by illegal behavior, one's mere racial association proves sufficient, such that many individuals must engage in the difficult act of proving their innocence.

While racial profiling is a tactic commonly associated with the police, the practice is understood as being more pervasive because it "is inextricably tied not only to race, but to [one's] conceptions of place, of what should typically occur in an area and who belongs, as well as where they belong" (Meehan & Ponder, 2002, p. 402). Therefore, Black Americans understand that wherever we go and whatever we do, there is a risk of having assumed criminality. We know that we can be profiled while shopping, bicycling, walking, taking a bus, boarding a plane, moving through customs, hailing a cab, or indeed any other scenario (Meehan & Ponder, 2002, p. 404). Independent of location, if we are perceived to being outsiders, those in power can exercise their privilege in determining whether we belong. Once again, born out of connections to the creation of the ideal slave, racial profiling requires its targets to obey and stay in *their* place while not acting too Black—a subversive attempt to metaphorically shackle individuals well over 150 years after the end of chattel slavery. Despite the progress made for advocates of Civil Rights, we are still vulnerable.

The actual practice of racial profiling is less about the racial intentions of the actor and more of an indictment of America's generalized perceptions about Black identity. The truth "is that people do not have to be racist—or have any malicious intent—in order to make decisions that unfairly harm members of another race" (Cose, 1993, p. 4). All that needs to happen is for people to believe, even just a little, that all Black Americans are predisposed to criminality. As a result, countless Americans, regardless of race, are guilty of making criminalized assumptions about Blackness, including Black Americans. Racial profiling does not only happen to Black people but through Black people. Therefore, White Americans, Asians, Latinos, *and* Black Americans can justify the humiliating presumptions of Black guilt because of cultural indoctrination and the dehumanizing assumptions that accompany Black American identity. Americans are socially conditioned to accept the dominant ideology about what it means to be Black (Banaji & Greenwald, 2013).

One of the many tragic results of this stereotype is that, while annual crime statistics repeatedly reveal that most Black Americans are noncriminals, they nonetheless feel as if they are in countless situations. As Cose (1993) noted:

> Rather than approach the matter of race and crime analytically, many perfectly intelligent people prefer to take an intellectually lazy path. Instead of analyzing the reality of the black threat, they focus only on the white fear; instead of assessing the soundness of various protective measures, they attempt to justify that fear and the discrimination motivated by it. (p. 109)

In other words, Black Americans are too often lumped into a racial collective, presumptively convicted for the transgressions of a tiny fraction of our racial brethren.

The experience of racial profiling epitomizes the trifecta of humiliation. Like a never-ending microaggression, targets are left powerless due to unjust treatment by the perpetrators, while witnesses rationalize the treatment and deny the unmistakable vulnerability of the targets. The belief is that if one would simply change his/her, behavior profiling would not occur. Comments are routinely offered, such as "Perhaps if you weren't in the wrong neighborhood, wore different clothes, drove a different car, were playing softer music or behaved in a different manner this would not have happened" or "If you didn't wear a hoodie, if you spoke more respectfully, or if you didn't walk around the store with those clothes in your hand you might have been able to avoid this." Deniers hold out hope that it's anything except racial profiling because an admission of such would violate their perception that the world, and most importantly our country, are fair and just.

Nearly every Black adult can share an experience of racial profiling and "there are few [among us] who don't have more than one story to tell" (Gates, 1995, p. 109). As Bell (1993) noted:

> Despite their undeniable progress no African Americans are insulated from incidents of racial discrimination. Our careers, even our lives, are threatened because of our color. Whatever our status we are feared because me might be one of "them." Success, then, neither insulates us from mis-identification by wary whites, nor does it ease our pain when we consider the plight of our less fortunate brethren. (p. 3)

While unjust, this is our lived experience and exemplifies the duality of our lives. It reminds us that becoming the victim of a humiliating act is inevitable. Professional ascendency and celebrity cannot insulate us from this experience. We know this because we frequently hear of these situations from celebrities such as Chris Rock (Saad, 2002), Oprah Winfrey (Reals, 2013), Danny Glover (Williams, 1999), James Blake (Goodman, 2015), Forest Whitaker (Lampard, 2013), Colin Powell (Hechtkopf, 2009), Tyler Perry (McEwen, 2012), Condoleeza Rice (Bumiller, 2009), Barack Obama (Obama, 2007), and Henry Louis Gates (Goodnough, 2009), to name just a few. While the context may differ, the list is endless; no matter how high we climb or who we become, our rightful place is always contested.

The Profiling of the Black Leader

While the concept of racial profiling is synonymous with assumptions about race and place, it should be noted that place is not exclusively limited to a physical location. Countless Black professionals and leaders understand that the racial stressors that plague our personal lives rarely disappear when we transition into our careers. Consequently, those of us who have obtained exclusive professional positions experience racial profiling in a way that is not dissimilar from how we experience it in our daily lives. Instead of being detained by police for absurd reasons like driving too slow or furtive movements, we find attempts being made by individuals who struggle with the idea of Black leadership, including those who are subordinate to us, to professionally apprehend our authority, especially when our leadership style collides with the status quo. Rather than being followed around a store where we do not appear to belong, we find our legitimacy being challenged, our authority utterly disregarded, and our ideas unnecessarily questioned or dismissed outright by those who hold similar beliefs.

This question of our belonging occurs because, to many, our professional status as leaders seems incongruent with our racial stereotypes (Barden, Maddux, Petty & Brewer, 2004; Eagley & Karau, 2002). The theory of role congruity (Eagley & Karau 2002) posits that members of stereotyped groups (e.g., racial minorities, women, etc.) who hold professional titles and counterstereotypic professional positions are more susceptible to prejudice. In other words, Black Americans' professional status in leadership positions conflicts with others' perceptions of their role in society. Therefore, when encountering a Black astronaut, chemical engineer, mathematician, professor, chief executive officer, doctor, or leader in virtually any capacity, many pause and marvel at these individuals as if they are unicorns, astonished at their ability to ascend to these prestigious positions while Black. The pause is typically followed by demands for justification: Whom we know, where we went to school, and what experiences we have had.

Consequently, many Black leaders who work in predominantly White environments seek to mitigate that role incongruity by putting on a professional mask to appear less stereotypically Black. Known as a working identity (Carbado & Gulati, 2015), this theory refers to people who feel coerced to behave in ways that conform to an organizations cultural norms and values. This is how individuals are pressured to "act White."

Some individuals might moderate the way they talk, dress, or wear their hair in an effort to appear less stereotypically Black. They might make it obvious that they are working late, attend happy hours against their wishes, or remain uncharacteristically silent on deeply personal issues in an effort to reduce the impact that perceptions of role incongruity might have on their role.

While the pressure to conform is more pronounced for individuals who are not White, in truth "everyone works their identity" (Carbado & Gulati, 2015, p. 69). Women, sexual minorities, religious minorities people of all races, and even white heterosexual men moderate their identities in their place of work to some degree because everyone desires to fit in. However, the pressure to work one's identity can be magnified when the employee is Black because of our obvious visibility in privileged professional spaces.

Despite attempts made by Black Americans to work our identities, we can never truly act White: Our minoritized status is too pronounced and the historical legacy of racial stereotypes, are too strong. Moreover, Black Americans do not have the same level of societal privilege as White Americans as our expressions of social vulnerability are different. One of the many privileges of being White in America is to have the ability to choose when to be vulnerable in a variety of societal contexts, whereas to be Black in this country is to live with that vulnerability being imposed. American history verifies that Black Americans are uniquely vulnerable. To suggest otherwise is to commit a postracial fallacy.

With this in mind, many Black employees will still attempt to work their identities and mitigate this vulnerability by trying not to appear *too Black*. Though this type of identity moderation occurs through the application many of the aforementioned practices it is found to happen most consistently through the limitation of one's speech (Carbado &

Gulati, 2015). While many in professional environments will quite naturally feel pressured to minimize the use of slang or code switch by minimizing the use of colloquialisms or vernacular, this dynamic of feeling coerced to moderate one's speech can have its most chilling effect when it comes to conversations about race.

Many Black Americans are aware that speaking too openly or honestly about racial issues in one's place of employment can lead one to being perceived as too militant or stereotypically angry, particularly in organizations that seek to promote a colorblind culture. Consequently, numerous Black Americans in professional environments may feel compelled to avoid conversations about race or racial discrimination all together. This occurs even when circumstances warrant because most know that when Black Americans take the risk by speaking too frankly about issues of racial inequality in one's place of employment can leave them vulnerable to attack. One of the many ways this assault manifests is through a collective form of bullying known as mobbing at work.

First coined by Leymann (1996), "The term *mobbing* delineates negative communicative actions, directed against an individual (by one or several others), and occurring very often and over a longer period of time" (Leymann, 1996, p. 21). Affecting those who are in a socially vulnerable position (Schuster, 1996), mobbing is a series of one or more of forty-five precisely defined actions (Table. 3.1) that "occur at least once a week over a period of half a year or more." (p. 272). The power of each of these aforementioned behaviors lies in their repetitive, long lasting, and humiliating nature. Virtually identical to microaggressions, these collective slights indicate that socially vulnerable targets do not belong (Leymann, 1996).

Table. 3.1—Forty-Five Elements of Mobbing.

Attacks on communication	Attacks on social relationship	Implications on social reputation	Attacks on the quality of professional and life situations	Attacks on health
• The boss limits opportunities to speak up. • Repeated interruptions. Colleagues limit opportunities to speak up. • Yelling or loud scolding. • Permanent critique of work. • Permanent critique of private life. • Telephone terror. • Oral threats. • Written threats. • Denial of contact by means of degrading looks or gestures.	• To stop talking to the person. • To not allow oneself to be addressed. • To relocate somebody far away from colleagues. • To forbid colleagues to address the person.	• Bad talk behind somebody's back. • Spreading rumors. • Ridicule. • To suspect somebody of being psychologically ill. • To try to force somebody to psychiatric examination. • Making fun of a handicap. • To ridicule by imitating movements, voice, or gestures. • To attack political or religious attitudes. • To make fun of the person's private life. • To make fun of the person's nationality. • To enforce carrying out work damaging to self-esteem. • To judge work in an improper or hurtful way.	• The person is not assigned any tasks. • The person is denied activity at the workplace, so that the person cannot even think of any task by him- or herself. • One assigns tasks that do not make any sense. • One assigns tasks far below the actual capabilities. • One permanently assigns new tasks.	• Health-threatening tasks enforced. • Physical aggression threatened. • Mild forms of violence used. • Physical abuse. • To cause costs for the person in order to harm him/her. • To cause physical damage at the home or workplace of the person.

Attacks on communication	Attacks on social relationship	Implications on social reputation	Attacks on the quality of professional and life situations	Attacks on health
•Denial of contact by means of allusions without directly addressing anything.	•To treat somebody as if not there.	•To doubt the decisions of the person. •To call him/her names or degrading expressions. •Sexual approaches or verbal sexual offers.	•One assigns tasks offending somebody's pride. •One assigns tasks far beyond the person's qualification to discredit him/her.	•Sexual violence (Schuster, 1996, pp. 310–311)

Source: Adapted from: "Rejection, exclusion, and harassment at work and in schools" by Schuster, B. 1996. *European Psychologist, 1*(4), pp. 310–311.

One of the most pernicious elements of mobbing is that the perpetrators seek to distort the reality of the target. Also known as gaslighting perpetrators of mobbing seek to intentionally manipulate the physical environment and mental state of their targets, by denying the deliberate nature of these actions, all in an effort to control their targets perception of reality (Roberts, & Carter Andrews, 2013). The mob ultimately hopes to maintain the position of truth-holder, defining not only the reality for the target but also that of any uniformed bystanders who might be unsure about the behaviors or actions of the target.

While mobbing at work can happen to anyone of any race, the practice of collective bullying can seem normal when directed toward Black Americans working in predominantly White environments because of our enhanced social vulnerability in these surroundings. No matter where we work or what role we have there is a strong likelihood that we will be in the minority. Moreover, the higher we climb on the professional ladder, the greater likelihood we are to have our minority status amplified. Therefore, Black Americans are easy targets for mobbing at work, especially when we refuse to work our identity.

Mobbing at work can prove to be particularly devastating when those who harbor superhuman stereotypes about Black Americans apply it. This is significant because the racial empathy gap that accompanies this stereotype creates the possibility for many of these practices may to be directed toward Black Americans at greater intensity levels and over greater periods of time than on individuals of other races based upon the assumption that the harm being imposed is not equally felt. Due to differing perceptions of empathy many find it hard to believe that Black Americans are inherently vulnerable or less capable of being wounded (Brown, 2012) despite the fact that all of our societal indicators reveal that Black Americans have an acute social vulnerability that is entirely unique.

Mobbing ultimately is an effort to terrorize minoritized individuals into behaving in ways that make those in the majority feel comfortable. What's more, this form of assault has a far-reaching effect, terrorizing not only the intended target but also anyone who shares the social identity of that target. A tactic used throughout American history (e.g., the lynch mob) mobbing is a collective effort to intimidate minoritized populations into remaining vulnerable, while discouraging sympathetic bystanders from intervening. In a way, mobbing is a collective effort to encourage people and groups to act White. Therefore, even if one finds the suggestion to moderate their behavior offensive, humiliating, and against one's values, the fear of mobbing at work creates a stronger incentive for someone to acquiesce when they otherwise would not.

This type of repression proves to be incredibly detrimental in the field of education because fearing conversations about race or speaking up for those who have historically disenfranchised only serves to continue the legacy of educational inequality for children in public schools. Having the freedom to speak an unfiltered truth about educational inequalities is essential if conditions of learning are to improve, however far too often the colorblind norms of many school systems prevent this from occurring.

Being one of the rare Black faces in a high-ranking space (Dyson, 2016) can at times feel like a battle against subversive attempts at personal and professional nullification. Analogous to numerous scenes in *Django Unchained*, we are left combatting constant attempts by a few individuals to disprove our exceptionality and knock us off our metaphorical horse. To them, it is inconceivable that we are qualified and deserve to be in our roles. Regardless of our field, title, or professional status, this is the reality that we face. We all have stories of the frustration and fatigue of living a life where our dignity is constantly under assault by a select few. "For most Blacks in America, regardless of status, political persuasion, or accomplishments, the moment never arrives when race can be treated as a total irrelevancy. Instead, too often it is the only relevant factor defining our existence" (Cose, 1993, p. 28).

The fact that we had to work twice as hard to get half as far is rarely considered. Instead, our successes are far too often rationalized by those who conceive of Black leadership as an unearned achievement bestowed by racial preference programs, lowered expectations, or diversity quotas;

to these individuals, our accomplishments are regarded as being incompatible with our race (Cose, 1993). Moreover, when it becomes clear that our talents and abilities cannot be legitimately dismissed, the attention then shifts to the authenticity of our Blackness. We receive backhanded compliments, such as "You're not really Black," and "You don't act like the other Black people I know." While illegitimate, repeated exposure to this type of manipulation of over an extended period of time still hurts, and leaves targets feeling gaslighted (Barton & Whitehead, 1969; Roberts & Carter Andrews, 2013) by the reality that they know to be true against the one their professional environment is trying to impose. These ongoing microaggressions against our professional status can feel demeaning and psychologically exhausting because we are constantly reminded "…that whatever [we] may accomplish in life, race remains [our] most salient feature as far as much of America is concerned" (Cose, 1993, p. 55).

Our Great Hope for a New Profile

Many Black Americans hoped that when Barack Obama was elected President of the United States, the effect of race would begin to hold less authority in the professional sphere. We knew that the Obama Presidency would represent the first time that most Americans would be led, albeit indirectly, by a Black man, giving us an opportunity to shift our collective racial profile from one of assumed criminals to leaders capable of shouldering the responsibility of guiding the most powerful country in the world. There were few of us who, on election night, did not believe that, as Sam Cooke sang, "a change is gonna come," allowing us to be seen as we saw ourselves. We all deeply felt that the presence of a Black Commander-in-Chief and First Family would diminish the automatic negative assumptions about Black criminality, thereby changing implicit perceptions of place. All the tears, shouts, wide-eyed smiles, and twinkles in our eyes during that time poignantly symbolized the possibility that we would finally be treated like human beings. Whether it was the moment when Barack Obama placed his left hand on the bible before a record-breaking inauguration crowd, or later that evening when Denzel Washington introduced a tearful Beyoncé at the Neighborhood Ball to sing the Etta James classic "At Last," we all exhaled with immense pride and held our heads higher. We knew that our country would never be the same.

Perhaps no symbol more perfectly captured the meaning of Barack Obama's presence than a photo taken on May 8, 2009 with five-year-old Jacob Philadelphia. The picture was made possible because Jacob's father, Carlton, worked at the White House as a staffer with the National Security Council under the George W. Bush Administration. Coinciding with the change in leadership, Carlton's two-year assignment to work at the White House was ending and he made the customary request for his family to have a picture taken with the President.

Carlton's wife Roseane and sons Isaac and Jacob were granted a brief visit with the President in the Oval Office. The photo of the Philadelphia family and Barack Obama was similar to those of other families who have posed with the President in front of the Resolute Desk. After the picture was taken, Isaac and Jacob were given an opportunity to ask the President a question. After Isaac first asked, "What was the next aircraft after the F-22?," White House photographer Pete Souza recalls the younger sibling, Jacob, initiating the following exchange:

> "I want to know if my hair is just like yours," he told Mr. Obama, so quietly that the president asked him to speak again.
>
> Jacob did, and Mr. Obama replied, "Why don't you touch it and see for yourself?" He lowered his head, level with Jacob, who hesitated.
>
> "Touch it, dude!" Mr. Obama said.
>
> As Jacob patted the presidential crown, Mr. Souza snapped.
>
> "So, what do you think?" Mr. Obama asked.
>
> "Yes, it does feel the same," Jacob said. (Calmes, 2012)

That exchange and the unforgettable image of a five-year-old Black American boy touching the hair of our nation's first Black President perfectly captured the emotion of many Black Americans and the symbolic importance of Barack Obama as our Commander-in-Chief.

That image took my breath away upon first glance (Figure 3.2). The dominant figure, standing in the center of a pristine Oval Office in front of the Resolute Desk, is five-year old Jacob. Dressed for the occasion, Jacob wears navy blue cargo pants and a white button-up shirt with a perfectly placed red-and-blue striped tie. His parents and older brother Isaac face him to his right, forcing the eye to remain fixed on Jacob and his slightly bent right hand, reaching to touch the head of the President, who bows low with hands in pockets.

What makes this picture (Figure 3.1) most memorable for me is the incredible intensity of Jacob's eyes as they look upon the President's hair. With his parents and brother obscured to his right and the President's eyes hidden as he bows, Jacob's eyes tell the story of the photograph. Even at five, Jacob's beautiful brown eyes, looking fervently upon the President's head as confirmation of his reality, perfectly convey the emotion and double consciousness that Black Americans live with daily. Asking the President of the United States if they had the same Caesar haircut was Jacob's five-year old way of asking if Barack Obama knew "how it felt to be a problem?" (Dubois, 1908/1994). As he placed his hand on the President's head in complete amazement, Jacob was looking for assurance that the most powerful man in the world knew what it felt like to be "an outcast and a stranger in his own house" (Dubois, 1908/1994, p. 2). Barack Obama provided that assurance for many Black Americans, including me.

However, shortly after that picture was taken, it became clear that, despite this historic moment, our country's racial habits (Glaude, 2016) had not changed. Although he'd received popular vote totals that reached unprecedented levels, the most powerful Black man in history (Dyson, 2016) was still profiled and met with the skepticism and suspicion that was all too familiar to many of us. While Barack Obama had credentials that was twice as good as most Americans' and had personal and professional story lines that were unassailable, our nation's first Black President gave the world a first-hand view of how Black professionals are profiled, mobbed, and coerced to perform a working identity within their places of work.

Figure 3.1—The White House.
Source: The White House/Pete Souza

Where the Office of the President of the United States was historically granted reverence and respect, in the presence of a Black Commander-in-Chief, the highest office in the most powerful country in the world now became a target of dehumanization and humiliation. Who could forget Representative Joe Wilson screaming "You lie!" when the President outlined his proposal for universal healthcare, or Governor Jan Brewer pointing her finger in the face of the Commander-in-Chief upon his arrival in Arizona? Both were widely considered unprecedented assaults on the dignity and integrity of the Office of the President of the United States, and yet the perpetrators were ultimately rewarded through increased fundraising by constituents. It became a pattern. We saw this later when Newt Gingrich called Obama the "food stamp president" (Elliott, 2012) and Representative Doug Lamborn used the phrase "tar baby" (Sherry, 2011) in reference to his opposition to the debt ceiling increase. We heard it from John Sununu, former Chief of Staff to George H. W. Bush, who called the President "lazy" after his first debate with Mitt Romney, and finally we witnessed it when former Governor of Alaska, Sarah Palin, stated that "Obama's shuck and jive ended with Benghazi lies" (Cirilli, 2012) amidst repeated cries by countless opponents to "take our country back." While veiled and indirect, each of these statements and actions allowed for plausible deniability by never specifically mentioning skin color, yet they indicated that, despite Obama's exceptionalism, he did not belong.

The racially coded appeals of dog whistle politics became standard fare in attacking our nation's first Black Commander-in-Chief and represented a new application of this strategy. Where racial grievance had historically been the exclusive domain of minoritized populations, the presence of a Black President and questionable assumptions about our post-racial identity encouraged complaints of racial intolerance by the White community. In doing so, dog whistle politics found a way to emphasize racial division while presenting "itself as a target of self-serving charges of racism" (López, 2013, p. 5). In an absurd twist, whenever our country's first President to have directly experienced racial discrimination spoke openly about race, he was immediately vilified for acknowledging the topic and thereby made the perpetrator of racism (Chasmar, 2014; Clegg, 2014). Talking about racial inequality made him *too Black*. This played out during the widely publicized racial profiling incident involving Henry Louis Gates, Jr. and the deaths of Trayvon Martin, Michael Brown, Eric Garner, Freddie Gray, and Tamir Rice. Whenever Obama acknowledged Black suffering or advocated for race-based policies designed to minimize our historical anguish, he was vigorously, repeatedly criticized as racist in an attempt to force him into a working identity. The objective was to keep the President silent on all matters that magnified racial inequality, while simultaneously holding him responsible for the maintenance of the racial status quo (Dyson, 2016). On matters of race, Obama could not win. Speaking openly about race brought accusations of racism, but if he avoided these conversations he was accused of trying to "act White" (Carbado & Gulati, 2015). This post-racial silencing strategy proved incredibly successful. Knowing that he would be challenged for whatever he did, Obama had to pick his poison. He could speak openly about race and risk not having any of his initiatives accepted, or avoid discussing issues that indicated his understanding of Black pain. Either way he lost, making it clear that, like me, our nation's first Black President was navigating the space between Carlton Banks and *Django Unchained*.

Reconciling My Miseducation

Prior to Obama's Presidency, I, like many others, cherished hopes for what his presence as our nation's leader might mean. However, the racial discrimination that permeated this country prior to the election of Barack Obama did not suddenly disappear. It simply changed into new forms to which many of us were blind. What I did not understand was that the Obama Presidency was never intended to be a marker of equity in our nation's long march toward equal justice; instead, it proved to be another "temporary peak of progress" (Bell, 1993, p. 64) in our country's efforts to manipulate the benefits of diversity. Although one of the most powerful men in history, Obama was not all that different from me when it came to an imposed working identity leading me to wonder if the Obama Presidency, like many other Civil Rights accomplishments in our nation's history, will be another in our country's long list of "short-lived victories that slide into irrelevance as racial patterns adapt in ways that maintain white dominance" (Bell, 1993, p. 12).

Now looking back on the entirety of the Obama administration, I can see how my thinking during his first election was naïve. Obama presidency was unsuccessful in substantially changing how Black leaders are perceived because the organizational culture of our government found a way to constrain his identity in a way that was not all that different from what many of us experience. Despite the fact that he handled these relentless attacks with a superhuman level of dignity and grace our voters still found a way to return our country to its typical racial habits by electing a successor to our first Black President who does not have to "act White" because he is.

This individual won the election by gaslighting the country, mercilessly bullying his political opponents and successfully creating a mob mentality, all while behaving in ways that magnified his wealthy White male heterosexual privilege. Obama's successor is a man who principally rose to political fame because of his attempts to humiliate our nation's first Black President by using many of the aforementioned mobbing techniques. Whether it was challenges to his citizenship, Christianity, academic qualifications, or professional accomplishments, the man elected President who followed Obama took full advantage of the moral credentials that the post-racial climate offered to diminish Obama's exceptionality and magnify his Blackness, while simultaneously directing assaultive speech toward women and racial and religious minorities. Obama's successor deployed the mobbing tactics with perfection and as a result was rewarded with the most powerful position on the planet.

If nothing else, observing this transition has taught me that attempts to keep me double consciousness will likely be permanent. No matter how high I climb in my professional station, no matter how many degrees I obtain or books I publish, assaults on my dignity will be ever-present. Professional success and personal accomplishment cannot absolve me of this. I could become President of the United States and yet I will never transcend race. I've realized that when my father-in-law said, "There are some people out there, regardless of race, who have a hard time being led by a Black person," he was really saying that there are some people who will never see you as you see yourself. Woodson noted, "Old men talk of what they have done, young men talk of what they are doing and fools talk of what they expect to do" (1933/2010, p. 64). Prior to the Obama Presidency, I was foolish because I was certain that with time, I could ensure that the people around me would see me in the way I saw myself. However, with maturity I realized that this desire to be seen in the way that I wish is not likely to always be fulfilled. In many ways, I learned to no longer stand on a corner waiting for things to change, but to accept my reality and learn to adjust.

References

Banaji, M. R., & Greenwald, A. G. (2013). *Blindspot: Hidden biases of good people.* New York, NY: Bantam Books.

Barden, J., Maddux, W. W., Petty, R. E., & Brewer, M. B. (2004). Contextual moderation of racial bias: The impact of social roles on controlled and automatically activated attitudes. *Journal of Personality and Social Psychology, 87*(1), 5.

Barton, R., & Whitehead, J. A. (1969). The gas-light phenomenon. *The Lancet,* 293(7608), 1258-1260.

Bumiller, E. (2009). *Condoleezza Rice: An American life: A biography.* New York, NY: Random House Incorporated.

Bell, D. A. (1993) *Faces at the bottom of the well: The permanence of racism.* New York, NY: Basic Books.

Calmes, J. (2012, May). When a boy found a familiar feel in a part of head of state. *New York Times.* Retrieved from http://www.nytimes.com/2012/05/24/us/politics/indelible-image-of-a-boys-pat-on-obamas-head-hangs-in-white-house.html

Carbado, D. W., & Gulati, M. (2013). *Acting white?: Rethinking race in post-racial America.* London: Oxford University Press.

Chasmar, J. (2014). Ben Stein: Obama "most racist president" in American history. *Washington Times.* Retrieved from http://www.washingtontimes.com/news/2014/nov/3/ben-stein-obama-most-racist-president-in-american

Cirilli, K. (2012, October). Palin defends "shuck and jive." *Politico.* Retrieved from http://www.politico.com/story/2012/10/palin-uses-racial-phrase-about-obama-082832#ixzz423hcpGh

Clegg, R. (2014, February) "My brother's keeper" and government-sponsored discrimination. *The National Review.* Retrieved from http://www.nationalreview.com/corner/372111/my-brothers-keeper-and-government-sponsored-discrimination-roger-clegg

Cose, E. (1993). *The rage of a privileged class: Why are middle-class Blacks angry? Why should America care.* New York, NY: HarperPerennial.

DuBois, W. E. B. (1994). *The souls of Black folk.* New York, NY: Dover Publications. (Original Work published 1903.)

Dyson, M. E. (2016). *The Black Presidency: Barack Obama and the Politics of Race in America.* New York, NY: Houghton Mifflin Harcourt.

Eagly, A. H., & Karau, S. J. (2002). Role congruity theory of prejudice toward female leaders. *Psychological review, 109*(3), 573.

Elliott, D. (2012, January 17). "Food stamp president": Race code, or just politics? *National Public Radio.* Retrieved from http://www.npr.org/2012/01/17/145312069/newts-food-stamp-president-racial-or-just-politics

Forgiarini, M., Gallucci, M., & Maravita, A. (2011). Racism and the empathy for pain on our skin. *Frontiers in Psychology, 2,* 108.

Gates, H. L., Jr. (1995, October 23). Thirteen ways of looking at a Black man. *The New Yorker*. Retrieved from http://www.newyorker.com/magazine/1995/10/23/thirt een-ways-of-looking-at-a-black-man

Goodman, J. D. (2015, October 8). Officer in James Blake arrest used excessive force, panel says. *New York Times*. Retrieved from http://www.nytimes.com/2015/10/08/ nyregion/officer-in-james-blake-arrest-used-excessive-force-panel-says.html

Goodnough, A. (2009, July 20). Harvard professor is jailed; officer is accused of bias. *New York Times*. Retrieved from http://www.nytimes.com/2009/07/21/ us/21gates.html

Hechtkopf, K. (2009, July 28). Powell says he has been racially profiled. *CBS News*. Retrieved from http://www.cbsnews.com/news/powell-says-he-has-been-rac ially-profiled/

Lampard, A. (2013, Aug. 23). Forest Whitaker recalls humiliating shoplifting snafu. *ABC News*. Retrieved from http://abcnews.go.com/blogs/entertainment/2013/08/ forest-whitaker-recalls-humiliating-shoplifting-snafu/

Leymann, H. (1996). The content and development of mobbing at work. *European Journal of Work and Organizational Psychology*, 5(2), 165–184.

López, I. H. (2013). *Dog whistle politics: How coded racial appeals have reinvented racism and wrecked the middle class*. New York, NY: Oxford University Press.

Meehan, A. J., & Ponder, M. C. (2002). Race and place: The ecology of racial profiling African American motorists. *Justice Quarterly*, 19(3), 399–430.

McEwen, L. (2012, April 6). Tyler Perry accuses cops of racial profiling. *Washington Post*. Retrieved from https://www.washingtonpost.com/blogs/therootdc/post/ tyler-perry-accuses-cops-of-racial-profiling/2012/04/06/gIQAh5v9zS_blog.html

Obama, B. (2007). *The audacity of hope: Thoughts on reclaiming the American dream*. New York, NY: Three Rivers Press.

Omi, M., & Winant, H. (2014). *Racial formation in the United States*. New York, NY: Routledge.

Ramirez, D., McDevitt, J., & Farrell, A. (2000). *A resource guide on racial profiling data collection: Promising practices and lessons learned*. Washington DC: U.S. Department of Justice.

Reals, T. (2013, Aug. 12). Oprah Winfrey says racism kept price bag out of her hands at Zurich, Switzerland shop. *CBS News*. Retrieved from http://www.cbsnews.com/ news/oprah-winfrey-says-racism-kept-pricey-bag-out-of-her-hands-at-zurich-switzerland-shop/

Roberts, T., & Carter Andrews, D. (2013). A critical race analysis of the gaslighting against African American teachers: Considerations for recruitment and retention. In D. J. C. Andrews & F. Tuitt (Eds.), *Contesting the myth of a "post-racial era": The continued significance of race in US education* (pp. 69–94). New York, NY: Peter Lang

Saad, N. (2009, April 2). Chris Rock's traffic stop selfies spark racial profiling discussion. *Los Angeles Times*. Retrieved from http://www.latimes.com/entertainment/

gossip/la-et-mg- chris-rock-third-traffic-stop-selfie-isaiah-washington-20150402-story.html

Schuster, B. (1996). Rejection, exclusion, and harassment at work and in schools. *European Psychologist, 1*(4), 293–317.

Sherry, A. (2011, August 2). Lamborn apologizes to Obama for "tar baby" remark. *Denver Post.* Retrieved from http://www.cbsnews.com/news/rep-lamborn-apologizes-after-tar-baby-remark/

Silverstein, J. (2013, June, 27 Day). I don't feel your pain: A failure of empathy perpetuates racial disparities. *Slate.* Retrieved from http://www.slate.com/articles/health_and_science/science/2013/06/racial_empathy_gap_people_don_t_perceive_pain_in_other_races.html

Trawalter, S., & Hoffman, K. M. (2016). Got pain? Racial bias in perceptions of pain. *Social and Personality Psychology Compass, 9*(3), 146–157.

Williams, M. (1999, November 4). Danny Glover says cabbies discriminated against him. *New York Times.* Retrieved from http://www.nytimes.com/1999/11/04/nyregion/danny-glover-says-cabbies-discriminated-against-him.html

Chapter 4

Leading While Black

We've got to give ourselves to this struggle until the end...We've got to see it through.

—*Martin Luther King, Jr., 1963*

Although stated earlier in this book, it bears repeating that educational leadership for educational equity is fundamentally complex and difficult work. At its core, this work "is not [about] mobilizing others to solve problems we already know how to solve, but to help them confront problems that have never yet been successfully addressed" (Fullan, 2014, p. 3). Through our work, we are literally trying to change history by accomplishing something that other sectors of society have yet to do. Therefore, as educators engage in this incredibly complicated task, we must rely on the long-held principles of leadership, such as goal setting, getting people in the right seats (Collins, 2001), consensus building, overcoming groupthink, and establishing trust to even have a chance at success. However, when we consider these activities in the context of our intersectional identities, our double consciousness, and the frequently unquestioned assumptions that surround them, it becomes clear that additional strategies need to be considered. That is, educational leadership for transformational change is not and has never been race-neutral.

Therefore, when I ask what it means to lead while Black, I am truly asking how our intersectional identities interfere with our ability to bring about transformational change for educational equity in our nation's public schools. How does the Black experience make our leadership challenges unique? Moreover, what are ways to successfully engage in this transformational work in Black bodies that are deliberately and subconsciously profiled in practically every sphere of American life? How do we do this in the face of stereotypical assumptions about our role congruity and attempts to silence our voice? How do we lead in a society that simply responds differently to Blackness? Finally, how do we contend with our double consciousness in bodies that are reflexively feared and misunderstood?

Fullan (2007) famously noted that "[e]ducational change depends on what teachers do and think—it is as simple and as complex as that" (p. 129). However, what he did not mention is that what teachers do and think is directly influenced by their feelings about their leaders. The perception of one's identity matters powerfully, having a direct impact on the simplicity or complexity of truly bringing about change. For Black school leaders, this means contending with stereotypes and assumptions because our minoritized status makes us appear to be cultural outsiders to parents, teachers, students and staff alike.

As Tschannen-Moran (2014) argued, "[i]ndividuals tend to attribute the motivations for the behavior of out-group members to differences in underlying attitudes or values, whereas with in-group members they are more likely to consider situational factors that might have influenced behavior" (p. 51). Because of their perceived difference, out-group leaders are less likely to be given the benefit of the doubt in their efforts to develop trust within the organization. Trust, as Bryk and Schneider (2002) noted, "is a critical component for successfully bringing about change in schools because it fosters a set of organizational conditions, some structural and others social-psychological, that make it more conducive for individuals to initiate and sustain the kinds of activities necessary to affect productivity improvements" (p. 161). Without it, change is not possible.

This additional hurdle makes Black educational leadership for transformative change decidedly more complex. Black educational leaders must not only overcome our status as out-group members and the role congruity that accompanies it, but we must do so in the face of constant skepticism about our motivations to improve the outcomes of our racial brethren. This creates a constant pressure to perform a working identity that does not appear *too Black* out of fear that we might become the target of mobbing. Our intersectional racial realities make our experiences in educational leadership different and, as a result, we must identify leadership methods that are reflective of our circumstances.

One of the places in the field where our minoritized status shows up most prominently is when it comes to perceptions of the cause of racial inequities in schools. For instance, studies have shown that Black educators are more likely to attribute the problem of educational inequity to issues within the school, whereas White educators are more likely to attribute the problem to the children (Vaught & Castagno, 2008; Uhlenberg, & Brown, 2002). Uhlenberg and Brown discovered that this phenomenon likely occurs because "no one likes to be blamed" (p. 522) for the problem. Taken together, this research reveals that Black educators do not want to believe that there is something inherent with the students, leading academic inequities, whereas White educators do not want to believe that their individual or collective decisions lead to these very same outcomes (Cobb, 2012).

When it comes to matters like these, it is likely that people will reach a conclusion about school inequity that aligns with their racial frame and assigns the least amount of blame to themselves, allowing them to preserve their sense of self. Lakoff (2004) noted that "frames are mental structures that shape the way we see the world" (p. xi). Often subconscious and automatic, frames provide rationale for the assumptions we make and the actions we take about any number of decisions in our lives. He continues, "You can only understand what the frames in your brain allow you to understand" (Lakoff, 2004, p. xiv).

When it comes to education, people will typically view inequality through one of three frames: deficit, diversity, or equity (Bensimon, 2005). Each frame has its own distinct characteristics and helps explain why ending racial inequity in schools can be so complex, even more so when the leader is Black.

A Problem of Framing for Educators

Educators who view educational inequity through the deficit frame believe in meritocracy and assume that the unequal outcomes in schools are directly attributable to the behaviors and decisions of students and their families. Therefore, they place the blame on the culture of poverty, lack of parental involvement, or a student's lack of motivation, desire, or grit, while ignoring the systemic factors in schools that contribute to unequal student outcomes (Bensimon, 2005). Deficit-minded thinkers from all racial groups defend their ideology by relying on stereotypical assumptions that have been normalized through cultural racism. They believe that unequal results are "natural in the light of the individuals' cultural, socioeconomic, and educational backgrounds" (Bensimon, 2005, p. 103) and that the only way to address these unequal results is to change the conduct of families and students. Deficit-minded thinkers deploy strategies, like parenting classes, remedial courses, and tutoring programs, that are aimed at correcting deficiencies believed to be inherent to the students and parents, while maintaining structures that contribute to these results. Consequently, since none of these strategies remedies the unequal results, this mindset represents a self-fulfilling prophecy that allows the deficit-minded to blame the victim.

Diversity-minded individuals, on the other hand, have a more positive approach but similarly limited success when addressing inequities. While they recognize that institutions bear some responsibility for unequal academic outcomes, they address the problem of inequity on the periphery. For educators who operate in the diversity frame, ensuring that students get access to broader forms of racial and cultural representation becomes the goal itself. Through this frame, individuals take pride in celebrating diversity and holding "workshops, sensitivity trainings, exposing whites to the 'other,' diversifying the curriculum" (Bensimon, 2005, p. 103), while not considering the institutional structures that produce the unequal outcomes. Applying what Banks (1993) regards and "the heroes and holidays approach," educators who apply the diversity frame are dysconscious (King, 1991) and believe they have a deeper understanding of educational equity than they do. They take steps to make students feel good, but do not take the critical step of changing the organizational structure to ensure that students are learning more. Diversity-minded individuals "are attuned to demographic differences...but more likely than not, they will be blind to the fact that the very students whose presence makes campus diversity possible are themselves experiencing unequal educational outcomes" (Bensimon, 2005, p. 102). Therefore, engaging in efforts that utilize the diversity frame can function as a form of plausible deniability by claiming that something is being done without engaging in the hard work of transforming an institution.

Finally, Bensimon (2005) believed that equity-minded individuals view school-based inequities as a shortcoming of the organization rather than the individuals experiencing the outcomes. Equity-minded individuals recognize that the problem of unequal outcomes is directly attributable to unequal treatment and not to the behaviors of students or the decisions that families make. Those who apply this frame have a heightened understanding of how "exclusionary practices, institutional racism, and power asymmetries impact opportunities and outcomes for Black and Latina/o students" (Bensimon, 2007, p. 446). Thus, those with an equity-minded frame look toward the actions of their colleagues, the organization, and themselves to identify the school-based structures that contribute to and inhibit student success. Equity-minded individuals are fundamentally committed to transforming the system and seek to do so by changing the frames of those with whom they work. We understand that "the problem of unequal outcomes resides... in [our] cognitive frames" (Bensimon, 2005, p. 100) and that, until those frames change, the results will likely be the same as well.

Therefore, how we talk about things matters. Although people use the words interchangeably, equity and diversity are not synonyms.

This distinction is critical because the aims of diversity do not match those of equity. The goal of equity is to bring about fairness and justice in the way that people are treated, whereas the purpose of diversity is simply to achieve difference within a group without consideration for the experience. Equity is concerned with equalizing the imbalance of power between groups, whereas diversity is simply concerned with representation, no matter how insignificant that might be. Therefore, when we use the language of diversity while trying to achieve equity, we are actually activating the frames of those we are trying to change by reinforcing their argument (Lakoff, 2004). To them, it sounds like we are focused on achieving the same goals when in truth we are not.

This is why the use of phrases such as "achievement gap," "low performers," or "economically disadvantaged" are discursively problematic when trying to describe the differences in performance between racial groups of students: They reinforce deficit and diversity frames by assuming that a student's academic standing is pathological instead of institutional. These phrases (especially the achievement gap) assume that learning experiences are equitable, denying the school's responsibility and placing the burden of performance exclusively on the student (Cobb & Russell, 2015). These terms assume that the students just aren't doing their part (Ladson-Billings, 2006).

Thus, when conversations focus on "the gap" between racial groups instead of the performance of all students relative to a goal, efforts to address the actual problem are undermined. This is why setting the right frame around this issue is so critical; if we fail to use the right terms to achieve true equity, we give subconscious license for educators to never change. However, changing one's cognitive frame is among the most challenging tasks in which we can engage because it presents an identity threat to those being challenged. To dismiss someone's frame as being incorrect is not simply to suggest that their thinking is wrong; rather, it is to assert that their identity is wrong. Questioning the basis for someone's frame can automatically lead to a sense of threat and deep resistance, as they attempt to stave off the shame that accompanies this challenge to their thinking (Brown, 2012).

Therefore, when teachers who share the deficit and diversity frames are confronted with the fact that unequal outcomes for racially minoritized students are directly attributable to inadequate curriculum, poor treatment of students, ineffective tutoring centers, or limited multicultural fairs, they are likely to internalize this message and regard it as an assault on their sense of self. This ultimately leads to psychological responses such as withdrawal, disengagement, defensiveness, and assuming the role of the victim. Educators will defensively ask, "Are you telling me I'm a bad teacher?" or "Are you saying I don't care about the success of my kids?" and "Are you calling me a racist?" all in an attempt to ward off their shame rather than accepting that their identity is wrong.

As Lakoff (2004) reminds us, "[y]ou can only understand what the frames in your brain allow you to understand. If the facts don't fit the frames in your brain, the frames in your brain stay and the facts are ignored or challenged or belittled (p xiv)" all in an effort to preserve the positive assumptions about one's identity. In instances like these, objective facts do not matter, only emotion that is further complicated by the legacy of America's unchallenged racial stereotypes.

This is why equity-minded leadership for transformational educational change while Black is so complex. As educators, we are almost always in the racial minority. Therefore, we must not only negotiate our thinking about educational leadership but the assumptions that others have about our intersectional identities while leading. Our Blackness and minoritized status in educational settings make it easy to dismiss our challenges to others' cognitive frames because we are easily identified as cultural outsiders who are difficult to trust (Tschannen-Moran, 2012) making us hyperaware of the decisions we make and the reactions that colleagues have toward them. We understand that our motivations for change are frequently met with skepticism.

Therefore, the ashamed often commit microaggressions in response to their feelings in an effort to mob us back into a more palatable working identity and frame. When we question an educational practice that disproportionately affects Black children (e.g., disciplinary practices, grades, or student achievement), educators with deficit or diversity frames are likely to rationalize their behaviors to preserve their identity by looking to dismiss our evidence on account of the individual offering it.

These realties, coupled with post-racial ideology and our role incongruity, makes our leadership realities distinct because we are required to navigate a space that other leaders do not. While we are committed to uplifting students who share our racial heritage, we are also regarded as being deserving of the reflexive humiliation that accompanies shame because we bear what James Baldwin termed the burden of representation (Gates, 1992).

Therefore, when we are observed in educational leadership roles by those who have a stereotypical cognitive frame about Black Americans, we are likely considered as being out of place and illegitimate, thereby confounding our ability to enact traditional leadership principles. The prevalence of long-held cultural stereotypes makes it easy for those who fail to question their validity to use them against Black Americans as weapons, even when we don't embody them. Therefore, even without deliberate racial intent, the ashamed often make us prime targets for microaggressions, humiliation, and mobbing so that we feel the same pain as the very students we are trying to support. Thus, equity-minded Black educational leaders are required to contend with the pain of double consciousness by splitting our emotional energy between the educational tasks at hand, while remaining hypervigilant to assaults to our dignity by subordinates. These are extra barriers that we have to overcome and leading in this context over a sustained period can become mentally exhausting, resulting in the physiological and psychological consequences called racial battle fatigue.

Racial Battle Fatigue

Smith, Allen, and Danley (2007) regarded racial battle fatigue as a theoretical framework for explaining the "strain exacted on racially marginalized groups and the amount of energy lost dedicated to coping with racial microaggressions and racism" (p. 555). A social condition, that could be considered as a response to gaslighting, racial battle

fatigue is regarded as an intense form of paranoia that occurs whenever Black Americans are forced to emotionally cope in cultural environments that are unsupportive, combative, and, at times, hostile.
This form of race-related stress is induced when we are required to
divert our energy toward disproving assumed racial stereotypes for
sustained periods of time. We suffer this strain out of a deep desire to
transcend race. The consequence of trying to maintain our dignity in
the face of what can feel like never-ending hostility leaves us emotionally exhausted, resulting in extreme physiological and psychological
responses (Table 4.1).

Table 4.1—Racial Battle Fatigue.

Physiological responses	Psychological responses
Tension headaches and back-aches	Constant anxiety and worrying
	Increased swearing and complaining
Elevated heart beat	Inability to sleep
Rapid breathing in anticipation of racial conflict	Sleep broken by haunting, conflict-specific dreams
	Intrusive thoughts and images
An upset stomach or "butter-flies"	Loss of self-confidence
	Difficulty in thinking coherently or being able to articulate (confirming stereotype)
Extreme fatigue	Hypervigilance
Ulcers	Frustration
Loss of appetite	Denial
Elevated blood pressure	John Henryism, or prolonged, high-effort coping with difficult psychological stressors
	Emotional and social withdrawal
	Anger, anger suppression, and verbal or non-verbal expressions of anger
	Keeping quiet
	Resentment

Source: Adapted from "Assume the position...you fit the description: Psychosocial experiences
and racial battle fatigue among African American male college students." by Smith, W. A., Allen,
W. R., & Danley, L. L., 2007. *American Behavioral Scientist*, 51(4), p. 556.

When enduring racial battle fatigue, we are constantly trying to
determine whether the stressors that we experience were "motivated
by a racist purpose, and how or if [we] should respond" (Smith, Allen,

& Danley, 2007, p. 557) to the humiliation that we're experiencing. Ironically, the relevance of the racial intent that leads to this form of race-related stress is immaterial because, as noted earlier in this book, racism feels like humiliation. However, labeling the motivations of our mistreatment as such in a professional environment, particularly in a post-racial climate, is politically risky because our claims of racism induce defensiveness and shame, thereby perpetuating the cycle (Brown, 2012). With this reality in mind, victims of racial battle fatigue become mentally weary as they perform their working identity, causing them to suffer in silent rage, paralyzed by the reality of their positionality. This constant debate and never-ending experience of double consciousness serves as an incredible distraction, making it virtually impossible to concentrate on our work.

Racial battle fatigue is known to most harshly affect Black Americans who have had greater professional success: those who are more educated, married, and have higher incomes (Smith, Hung, & Franklin, 2012). This is because we are the ones who feel that we have earned the right to be treated with deference and courtesy because of our professional accomplishments. We've made the right choices and played by society's rules; because of that, we feel entitled to be judged on the content of our character and to be seen as we see ourselves. We *should* transcend race.

Therefore, when we're confronted with situations that appear racially motivated, it feels incongruent with how we expect to be treated. To have our guilt presumed, our motivations questioned, and our ideas constantly challenged heightens our double consciousness and reminds us that, despite our professional ascendancy and accomplishments, we are not above humiliation. The fact that we cannot control this unjust treatment, and yet believe that it should be within our power to do so, leaves us utterly exhausted and asking: What have I done to deserve this?

Equity-minded Black educational leaders are prime candidates for racial battle fatigue. We embody the typology of the individuals mentioned above. Moreover, transformational change is fraught with conflict and, consequently, educators resist the shame that they experience in ways that feel personal because "shame can only rise so far in a system before people disengage and protect themselves" (Brown, 2012, p. 192). This type of resistance can lead Black educators to ask whether the personal attacks are, in fact, racially motivated. Therefore, when we encounter efforts to maintain the status quo and preserve Black students' academic suffering, we question the implicit and explicit racial motivations of the resisters. These are *our* children and the inhumanity of their collective suffering seems obvious because we know that Black children have done nothing to deserve their treatment. Our inability to quickly overcome this resistance can be frustrating. Nonetheless, we begin our task with a firm sense of hope and a belief that we can bring about transformational change in our schools.

Smith, Hope, and Franklin (2012) argued, "hope is like a pendulum" (p. 49); it can magnify or diminish the physiological and psychological stress that accompanies racial battle fatigue. While hope might prove beneficial in other avenues of life, it can be psychologically and physiologically devastating in the context of racial discrimination. The hope that we can bring about transformational change in our systems also leads to the racial stress that makes us believe our efforts are for naught. The hope that sustains us and leads us to believe that, with little resistance, we can make an entire school community more equity-minded also leads to exhaustion. Ultimately, that hope is naïve.

Freire (1997) reminds us "[t]he idea that hope alone will transform the world, and action undertaken in that kind of naïveté, is an excellent route to hopelessness, pessimism, and fatalism" (p. 8). Naïve hope is what leads to racial battle fatigue because we believe that we should be able to overcome racism. Ladson-Billings (2015) reminded us, however, that in our commitment to end Black academic suffering, we must remember that "we are not in this fight to win, we are in this fight to struggle." Therefore, we must commit to that struggle and identify adaptive coping strategies in the face of constant exposure to unjust treatment. I argue that we must do this by accepting the realities of our racial positionality in educational leadership and in what Bell (1992) identified as racial realism.

Racial Realism

Like our acceptance of racial profiling, racial realism is the fundamental acknowledgment that Black Americans throughout history have occupied a subordinate social status despite their many accomplishments. Whether it is through desegregation, attending a school, or even becoming the President of the United States, Black Americans remain the faces at the bottom of society's well (Bell, 1992). Racial realists accept the fact that racism is a central and historical structure of American society rather than a collection of hate-filled individuals.

Racial realism does not mean accepting the assumptions that undergird the deficit ideology; rather, it is an acknowledgment that we are likely always to encounter those who hold it. While this approach can at first seem fatalistic, racial realists note that our likelihood to encounter racial discrimination "is as true as is the seldom acknowledged fact that each of us is going to die" (Bell, 2005, p. 89). Therefore, as racial realists "we seek the salvation in life that comes when we accept the reality of death" (Bell, 2005, p. 89) and believe that "as a matter of faith…that, despite the lack of linear progress, there is satisfaction in the struggle itself. The fight in itself has meaning and should give us hope for the future" (Bell, 1992, p. 98). With the racial realist approach, we adopt the work from Hope, Smith, and Franklin (2012), avoiding despair by taking a more realistic approach when encountering racial discrimination and resistance toward transformative educational change. We take the long view, and expect resistance as a part of our lived experience because engagement in struggle is the Black American story and we know:

> This engagement and commitment is what Black people have had to do since slavery: making something out of nothing. Carving out humanity for oneself with absolutely nothing to help—save imagination, will, and unbelievable strength and courage. Beating the odds while firmly believing in, knowing as only they could know, the fact that all those odds are stacked against them… (Bell, 1992, pp. 198)

Unlike those who succumb to racial battle fatigue, we are committed to the struggle, as opposed to simply behaving as reluctant participants who believe that "we shall overcome." We know that role incongruity, distrust, skepticism, and incongruent frames are simply a part of the experience and use this knowledge as psychic armor to counteract it. This refusal to be surprised by discrimination when we encounter it gives us the ability to persist and diminishes the constant pain of double-consciousness because we are less affected by the way we see ourselves in others. In "taking away the gaze" (Leve, 2012) of those who accept the validity of long held stereotypes, we are more freely able to live beyond the veil of race, reclaim our dignity, and "merge [our] double self into a better and truer self" (Dubois, 1903/1994, p. 2).

For this reason, I have developed a theoretical framework for transformational change, called Leading While Black (LWB), which takes the racial realities of equity-minded Black education leaders into account. The LWB (Figure 4.1) is composed of three fundamental principles: equity mindedness, racial battle fatigue, and racial realism. These concepts are organized deliberately around an isosceles triangle, in which two of the three sides are equal.

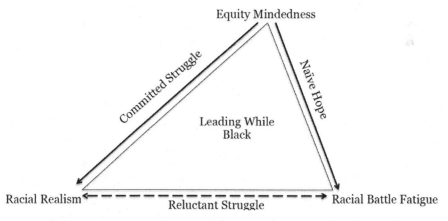

Figure 4.1—Leading While Black Theoretical Framework.

The starting point of the LWB framework is commitment to equity-mindedness and the belief that striving toward educational equity is a necessary, meaningful pursuit in public education. However, when engaging in efforts to achieve educational equity, leaders can take one of two approaches to achieve these ends. When Black equity-minded educational leaders approach transformational educational change with naïve hope, believing there will be no struggle, the physiological and psychological symptoms that accompany it are inevitable. Racial realism can be achieved via this approach, but not without reconciling one's double consciousness. Because of this, the pathway to racial realism is not dissimilar to the others. Conversely, when equity-minded leaders strive toward educational equity with anticipation that struggle is fundamental to this work, we allow ourselves to achieve a racial realism that supports us in understanding that "continued struggle can bring about unexpected benefits and gains that in themselves justify continued endeavor" (Bell, 2004, p. 192). Through this path, we know the struggle *is* real.

As racial realists, we have a keen sense of history and deploy racial realism, knowing that public schools have never been equitable spaces (Burris & Garrity, 2008). Racial realists understand the Interest Convergence tenet of Critical Race Theory, which posits that, historically, "the interest of Blacks in achieving racial equality have been accommodated only when they have converged with the interests of powerful whites" (Bell, 1995, p. 22). Interest convergence is as much a psychological principle as it is theoretical, relying on the philosophical concept of psychological egoism (Litowitz, 1996) and the principle of enlightened self-interest (Secada, 1989), both of which assert that human beings are fundamentally motivated by self-interest. Therefore, when confronting change, human beings are predisposed to ask, "What is in this for me?" because "power concedes nothing without a demand, it never did and it never will" (Douglass, 1857, p. 367).

When considering interest convergence in the context of transformational change for educational equity, it's important to note that some educators and parents are interested in maintaining the status quo because, despite its inequities, it provides a benefit. For certain educators, self-interest rests in maintaining their teaching loads, the student composition of their courses, and their buildings. This reality is again what makes the diversity frame so palatable: It gives the appearance of change on the periphery without fundamentally addressing anything structural at the core. In doing so, the diversity frame offers a moral credential to educators who believe that they at least did something, although those efforts produce little to no results.

Some privileged parents have an aversion toward educational change because they view education as a competition for limited resources. Since the current system works for them and their children, they have little incentive for change. However, in addition to interest convergence, these parents also rely on the lesser-known concept of interest divergence (Gillborn, 2013; Guinier, 2004), which seeks to maintain historical social class and racial hierarchies. Supported by the Nietzschean concept of will to power (1968), the theory of interest divergence posits that human beings have a fundamental desire to maintain dominance over others. Therefore, when equity-related reforms are recommended to privileged parents, some will likely demand the continuation of a stratified system because they want their children to maintain their relative social standing over others (Wells & Oakes, 1996). Lucas (2001) referred to this phenomenon as *effectively maintained inequality*. The theory posits, "that socioeconomically advantaged actors secure for themselves and their children some degree of advantage wherever advantages are commonly possible" (p. 1652), thus complicating any effort to close opportunity gaps in schools. When efforts become focused on creating opportunities for historically disadvantaged students, these parents will demand additional opportunities for their children to keep the social hierarchy in place.

Interest convergence and interest divergence present an inconvenient truth for those committed to transformational change for educational equity because, despite frequent claims to the contrary, not everyone is truly interested in equal access for all students. This is further complicated when the individual championing the initiative is from a racial group that will benefit from the proposed change, because privileged parents often view education as a game of winners and losers. This, again, is why leading while Black can be such a challenge: Our efforts to end the institutional suffering of underserved students can far too often be perceived as an effort to simply subordinate the privileged students. While it can certainly feel unfair that our leadership path is different from that of others, this is the context in which we are required to lead.

However, accepting this truth allows us to commit to the struggle and construct new strategies for success instead of believing naively that our reality will somehow change. When devising approaches to confront this reality, we must caution against our natural impulse to confront the historical oppression of underserved children by recreating structures of oppression (Freire, 1997). Fighting humiliation with humiliation serves only to reinforce the methods of the privileged and deficit-minded, keeping underserved students firmly in their place. Instead, we must support the leadership model of academic inclusivity by advocating to equalize a power structure that has been institutionally tilted against disenfranchised communities. We do so, in the words of King, (1968), "by appealing to the conscience of the great decent majority who through blindness, fear, pride, and irrationality have allowed their consciences to sleep." This is the essence of the civil rights struggle and, as leaders committed to educational equity, is our struggle as well.

References

Bell, D. A. (1992). *Faces at the bottom of the well: The permanence of racism.* New York, NY: Basic Books.

Bell, D. A. (1995) Brown v. Board of Education and the interest convergence dilemma. In K. Crenshaw & N. Gotanda (Eds.). *Critical race theory: Key writings that formed the movement* (pp. 20–29). New York, NY: Routledge.

Bell, D. A. (2004). *Silent covenants: Brown v board of education and the unfulfilled hopes for racial reform.* Cambridge: Oxford University Press.

Bell, D. A. (2005). Racism is here to stay now what. In R. Delgado & J. Stefancic (Eds.). *The Derrick Bell Reader* (pp. 85–90). New York, NY: NYU Press.

Bensimon, E. M. (2005). Closing the achievement gap in higher education: An organizational learning perspective. *New Directions for Higher Education, 131,* 99.

Banks, J. A. (1993). Multicultural education: Historical development, dimensions, and practice. *Review of research in education, 19,* 3–49.

Bensimon, E. M. (2007). The underestimated significance of practitioner knowledge in the scholarship on student success. *The Review of Higher Education, 30*(4), 441–469.

Brown, B. (2012). *Daring greatly: How the courage to be vulnerable transforms the way we live, love, parent, and lead.* London: Avery.

Burris, C. C., & Garrity, D. T. (2008). *Detracking for excellence and equity* [eBook]. Retrieved from http://www.ascd.org/publications/books/108013.aspx

Bryk, A. S., & Schneider, B. (2003). Trust in schools: A core resource for school r reform. *Educational Leadership, 60*(6), 40–45.

Cobb, F. (2012). *It's About Access: How the Curricular System and Unequal Learning Opportunities Predict The Racial Test Score Gap In Mathematics* (Doctoral dissertation, University of Denver. Retrieved from http://digitalcommons.du.edu/cgi/viewcontent.cgi?article=1783&context=etd.

Cobb, F., & Russell, N. M. (2014). Meritocracy or complexity: Problematizing racial disparities in mathematics assessment within the context of curricular structures, practices, and discourse. *Journal of Education Policy 30*(5), 631–649.

Collins, J. (2001). *Good to great: Why some companies make the leap...and others don't.* New York, NY: Harper Collins Publishers.

Douglass, F. (1857). West India emancipation speech. In P. S. Foner (Ed.), *Frederick Douglass: Selected speeches and writings* (pp. 358–368). Chicago, IL: Lawrence Hill Books.

Fullan, M. (2007). *The new meaning of educational change.* New York, NY: Routledge.

Fullan, M. (2014). *Leading in a culture of change personal action guide and workbook.* New York, NY: John Wiley & Sons.

Freire, P. (1997). *Pedagogy of the Oppressed.* New York, NY: Continuum.

Fullan, M. (2007). *The new meaning of educational change.* New York, NY: Routledge.

Gates, H.L. (1992). From the stacks: The fire last time. *New Republic.* Retrieved from: https://newrepublic.com/article/114134/henry-louis-gates-james-baldwin-fire-last-time

Gillborn, D. (2013). Interest-divergence and the colour of cutbacks: Race, recession and the undeclared war on black children. *Discourse: Studies in the Cultural Politics of Education, 34*(4), 477–491.

Guinier, L. (2004). From racial liberalism to racial literacy: Brown v. Board of Education and the interest-divergence dilemma. *The Journal of American History, 91*(1), 92–118.

King, J. E. (1991). Dysconscious racism: Ideology, identity, and the miseducation of teachers. *The Journal of Negro Education, 60*(2), 133–146.

Ladson-Billings, G. (2006). From the achievement gap to the education debt: Understanding achievement in US schools. *Educational researcher, 35*(7), 3–12.

Ladson-Billings, G. (2015, April, 8). Critical race theory and education [Video file]. Retrieved from https://www.youtube.com/watch?v=katwPTn-nhE

Lakoff, G. (2004). *Don't think of an elephant!: Know your values and frame the debate.* New York, NY: Chelsea Green Publishing.

Leve, A. (2012, July 7). Tony Morrison on love loss and modernity. *The Telegraph.* Retrieved from: http://www.telegraph.co.uk/culture/books/authorinterviews/9395051/Toni-Morrison-on-love-loss-and-modernity.html

Litowitz, D. E. (1996). Some critical thoughts on critical race theory. *Notre Dame Literature Review, 72*, 503.

Nietzsche, F. (1968). *The will to power.* New York, NY: Random House.

Secada, W. G. (1989). Agenda setting, enlightened self-interest, and equity in mathematics education. *Peabody Journal of Education, 66*(2), 22–56.

Smith, W. A., Allen, W. R., & Danley, L. L. (2007). "Assume the position...you fit the description": Psychosocial experiences and racial battle fatigue among African American male college students. *American Behavioral Scientist, 51*(4), 551–578.

Smith, W. A., Hung, M., & Franklin, J. D. (2012). Between hope and racial battle fatigue: African American men and race-related stress. *The Journal of Black Masculinity, 2*(1), 35–58.

Tschannen-Moran, M. (2014). *Trust matters: Leadership for successful schools.* New York, NY: John Wiley & Sons.

Uhlenberg, J., & Brown, K. M. (2002). Racial gap in teachers' perceptions of the achievement gap. *Education and Urban Society, 34*(4), 493–530.

Vaught, S. E., & Castagno, A. E. (2008). "I don't think I'm a racist": Critical Race Theory, teacher attitudes, and structural racism. *Race Ethnicity and Education, 11*(2), 95–113.

Wells, A. S., & Oakes, J. (1996). Potential pitfalls of systemic reform: Early lessons from research on detracking [Extra issue]. *Sociology of Education, 69,*135–143.

Chapter 5

Still Fighting for Freedom: #BlackLeadershipMatters

To live is to wrestle with despair, yet never let despair have the last word

—*Cornel West, 2014*

Lessons Learned

My perspectives have matured since I entered educational leadership, although I still feel that I know nothing compared to my father-in-law. I entered the field of school leadership with a naïve understanding of the daily struggle I would face as a Black equity-minded leader committed to closing the opportunity gap. While I have made some progress in adjusting the cognitive frames of many of those with whom I work to increase life and academic opportunities for underserved children, it needs to be noted that this progress (albeit minor) has not been possible without a fight. Every step toward equity has been met with new and unique ways to resist because despite many of the often stated proclamations, education is a field with individuals who have a number of competing interests, many of which work against equity.

When I entered into school leadership, I was under the impression that our issues of school inequality could be addressed quickly not fully understanding how deeply connected they were to many of the other inequities facing our country. The resistance to equal treatment we observe in education is not all that different from opposition we see in every other element of society, therefore it should not come as a surprise that our efforts to overcome this reality is so incredibly difficult. As much as it hurts to admit this, I now understand that "the impossible will take a while" (Loeb, 2014, p. 4). Though I was incapable of understanding this at the time, this was what my father-in-law was trying to tell me all along: Black leadership for educational equity is a constant struggle. I need to do everything I can do to improve the conditions for students and then one day be prepared to pass that legacy on to someone else.

The fatal mistake that I made, one that I believe that many aspiring leaders make when they enter leadership roles, was that I assumed that Black leadership for educational equity was supposed to be easy. In a way, this seems natural, because those who are incredibly skilled at using their gift have the ability to make what they do look easy, despite the difficulty of the task. We question why certain decisions are made and why they didn't do more with their time as leaders; unaware of the resistance they faced to accomplish the things they did. We've seen this a lot in the criticisms of the Presidency of Barack Obama, as so many hoped that he would accomplish more related to social inequality than he did because he made leadership look easy.

What's clear to me now is that when we blame Black leaders for not doing enough to eradicate centuries of racial inequality, we succumb to the postracial trap of ignoring the unique vulnerability of Black Americans. More importantly, we fall victim to the same logic of respectability politics that we so vigorously despise whenever we find ourselves the victims of race-based discrimination. In both instances, it is assumed that a change in our personal behavior would have resulted in a difference in treatment because both are attempts at rationalization that apply the just world fallacy. Truthfully, we should apply skepticism when Black leaders are criticized for "not doing enough" just as we do when challenged about our efforts to reduce Black-on-Black crime. Both dismiss the possibility of Black vulnerability in the moment.

This was what I could not understand about my father-in-law's efforts to address inequality in his school. In my profound admiration for him, I failed to understand his immense social vulnerability. My assumptions about the benefits that came with the authority of his title blinded me to his obvious racial susceptibility. As someone whose childhood's critical moments were defined by this, I should have known better. My experience with vulnerability as a child was no different from what he lived with professionally every day, because firsts and onlys are inherently vulnerable.

The truth is, when we make the decision to address educational equity we are not signing up for easy, we are signing up for struggle. This was the reality of our ancestors who led the charge to end inequality in all forms. Leading while Black is hard. However, as Barack Obama reminded us in his 2011 annual address to the Congressional Black Caucus:

> ...more than a lot of other folks in this country, we know about hard...And we don't give in to discouragement.
>
> Throughout our history, change has often come slowly. Progress often takes time. We take a step forward, sometimes we take two steps back. Sometimes we get two steps forward and one step back. But it's never a straight line. It's never easy. And I never promised easy. Easy has never been promised to us. But we've had faith. We have had faith. We've had that good kind of crazy that says, you can't stop marching.
>
> Even when folks are hitting you over the head, you can't stop marching. Even when they're turning the hoses on you, you can't stop. Even when somebody fires you for speaking out, you can't stop. Even when it looks like there's no way, you find a way—you can't stop. Through the mud and the muck and the driving rain, we don't stop. Because we know the rightness of our cause—widening the circle of opportunity, standing up for everybody's opportunities, increasing each other's prosperity. We know our cause is just. It's a righteous cause. (Obama, 2011)

To walk this path correctly, we are destined to spend our careers in struggle. We know this is the case because this is how the Black American march toward equality has been defined. Our story is one of resilience that does not always lead to all of the outcomes that we seek. Our efforts, no matter how committed we are to them, "are not likely to lead to transcendent change and may indeed, despite our best efforts, be of more help to the system we despise than to the victims of that system whom we are trying to help" (Bell, 1992, p. 198). Nonetheless, we know that our presence serves "to remind the powers that be that out there are persons like us who are not only not on their side but determined to stand in their way" (Bell, 1992, pp. 198–199).

Therefore, as we are symbolically passed the baton and begin to shoulder that burden of leadership for educational equity, we must never forget that the fight to end racial inequality has never been easy. However, despite the challenges that this work has always presented, we must remember that our struggles will never be greater than those of our ancestors. They fought, suffered, and died so that we could be privileged enough to have this struggle.

When confronted with resistance in our efforts to end Black suffering, we must do our best to reinterpret that pushback as a badge of honor because this work has never been easy. However difficult it may be, we must remain resolute, use our voices to speak truth and remember that many of the people (regardless of race) who blame us for our lack of progress in achieving educational change are the very people who stand in our way. If nothing else, the eight years of the Obama administration have taught us that. However, it is that resilience in the face of constant struggle that makes the Black American story incredibly special. We have always beaten the odds, even though they are always stacked against us (Bell, 1992). Baldwin (1985) reminded us that, "We are capable of bearing a great burden, once we discover that the burden is reality and arrive where reality is" (p. 372). If we are sincere in our efforts to achieve those ends, we are better served to come to that reality.

To you young Black leaders, who are committed to improving the academic experiences of Black children in your schools and districts, remember that your work is not going to be easy. However, in spite of the constant struggle and mind-numbingly slow pace of change, know that your presence matters, your endurance matters, and most importantly, this type of Black leadership matters. It matters to the parents who know that you are fighting for their children. It matters to young teachers who are inspired by your example and it matters to the children, such as Jacob Philadelphia, who look up to us with beautiful, hopeful eyes. Dr. King (1964) reminds us:

> …before we reach the majestic shores of the Promised Land, there is a frustrating and bewildering wilderness ahead. We must still face prodigious hilltops of opposition and gigantic mountains of resistance. But with patient and firm determination we will press on…

Emerging and aspiring leaders, we must press on!

References

Baldwin, J. (1985). *The fire next time*. New York, NY: Vintage.

Bell, D. A. (1992). *Faces at the bottom of the well: The permanence of racism*. New York, NY: Basic Books.

King M. L., Jr. (1964). *Nobel Lecture*. Retrieved from http://www.nobelprize.org/nobel_prizes/peace/laureates/1964/king-lecture.html

Loeb, P. (2014). *The impossible will take a little while: A citizen's guide to hope in a time of fear*. New York, NY: Basic Books.

Obama, B. H. (2011, March 4). Remarks by the President at congressional black caucus foundation annual phoenix awards dinner. Retrieved from https://www.whitehouse.gov/the-press-office/2011/09/24/remarks-president-congressional-black-caucus-foundation-annual-phoenix-a

West, C. (2014). Prisoners of hope. In Loeb, P. (Ed.), *The impossible will take a little while: A citizen's guide to hope in a time of fear*. New York, NY: Basic Books.

ROCHELLE BROCK & CYNTHIA DILLARD
Executive Editors

Black Studies and Critical Thinking is an interdisciplinary series which examines the intellectual traditions of and cultural contributions made by people of African descent throughout the world. Whether it is in literature, art, music, science, or academics, these contributions are vast and far-reaching. As we work to stretch the boundaries of knowledge and understanding of issues critical to the Black experience, this series offers a unique opportunity to study the social, economic, and political forces that have shaped the historic experience of Black America, and that continue to determine our future. Black Studies and Critical Thinking is positioned at the forefront of research on the Black experience, and is the source for dynamic, innovative, and creative exploration of the most vital issues facing African Americans. The series invites contributions from all disciplines but is specially suited for cultural studies, anthropology, history, sociology, literature, art, and music.

Subjects of interest include (but are not limited to):

- EDUCATION
- SOCIOLOGY
- HISTORY
- MEDIA/COMMUNICATION
- RELIGION/THEOLOGY
- WOMEN'S STUDIES

- POLICY STUDIES
- ADVERTISING
- AFRICAN AMERICAN STUDIES
- POLITICAL SCIENCE
- LGBT STUDIES

For additional information about this series or for the submission of manuscripts, please contact Dr. Brock (University of North Carolina at Greensboro) at r_brock@uncg.edu or Dr. Dillard (University of Georgia) at cdillard@uga.com.

To order other books in this series, please contact our Customer Service Department:

(800) 770-LANG (within the U.S.)
(212) 647-7706 (outside the U.S.)
(212) 647-7707 FAX

Or browse online by series at www.peterlang.com.